Diveheart Adaptive Diver Training Manual

DIVEHEART

© First Edition February 2014 by Diveheart. No part of this book may be reproduced, stored in a retrieval system or transmitted in any form or by any means without the prior written permission of the publishers, except by a reviewer who may quote brief passages in a review to be printed in a newspaper, magazine or journal.

Copyright © 2014 Diveheart

All rights reserved.

ISBN-13: 978-0-9885058-3-4

DEDICATION

We dedicate this to the spirit of those with disabilities who dare to imagine the possibilities in their lives.

"Diveheart has done a tremendous job capturing both the practical aspects as well as the passion of adaptive diver training in their new instructional materials. As dive professionals, we have the privilege of introducing people of all ilk to the underwater world, but it's a humbling experience to provide this opportunity to those that might not otherwise be given the chance to step beyond their perceived boundaries. Scuba diving is the true equalizer and the Diveheart training program opens this door for you to share in this journey with these future scuba divers."

> Jeff Myers, COO, Health & Safety Institute
> PADI Course Director
> Former COO & VP of Training, DAN
> Former Manager, Training, Education and Memberships, PADI

"I am amazed at the clarity and compassion projected throughout the documents."

> Peter Meyer
> Willis Insurance
> Recreational Dive Programs

"The training manual is a wonderful advance. When Jim Elliot says "imagine the possibilities" he really means it. He is not deterred from taking on even the most challenging problems faced by divers with varying levels of abilities. The Duke Center for Hyperbaric Medicine and Environmental Physiology is proud to be able to offer medical consultation and research guidance to Diveheart as it pursues its goals of offering training to divers of all levels, particularly those injured during military service."

> Jake Freiberger, MD, MPH
> Associate Professor of Anesthesiology
> Duke Center for Hyperbaric Medicine & Environmental Physiology
> Executive Director of Duke Dive Medicine
> Duke University Medical Center

TABLE OF CONTENTS

Acknowledgments i

Special Acknowledgment 1

The Diveheart Program Development Team 3

Chapter 1: Introduction 7

    Philosophy, Program Description and Goals 8

Chapter 2: DIVEHEART'S ADAPTIVE DIVE Team Approach and YOUR Responsibility to Share Information 11

Chapter 3: Needed Scuba Assistance (NSA) Evaluation: 14

    An Emphasis on Key Scuba Skills for Safety 16

    Ongoing Evaluation and the Final NSA Course Evaluation 17

    Self-NSA Assessments Post Certification—Your Continuing Responsibility 18

    Diveheart's Post Certification NSA Commitment 18

Creating an Adaptive Diver's Profile 18

Chapter 4: ENHANCED Buddy System—*The Adaptive Dive Team* 20

Adaptive Diver's Responsibility to Communicate Special Modifications and Needed Assistance. 21

The Roles of Your Adaptive Dive Buddies 23

Primary and Secondary Roles of the Adaptive Dive Team 23

Predive Briefings with the Adaptive Dive Team 24

Chapter 5: Learning Adaptive diving 27

Independent study program 27

Performing Scuba Skills with Adaptations 28

Special Adaptations, Techniques, Procedures and Team Work—for the Performance of Scuba Skills 29

Improvise, Adapt, Overcome and Conquer Scuba Skills 32

Diving system assembly and disassembly 33

Equipment inspection (at water's edge) 36

Adaptive Equipment Inspections 38

Donning and Removing Scuba Gear 45

Entries and exits 52

Proper weighting 64

Weight/ballast system- underwater removal and replacement 71

Mouthpiece clearing - snorkel and regulator 73

Regulator/snorkel exchanges and Surface Swimming 76

Underwater "Gravity Free" Swimming 78

Hand signals for Visually-Impaired Divers 88

Underwater navigation 91

Mask-clearing, including removal and replacement 92

Regulator Recovery/ Retrieval 95

Buddy-system techniques 98

Diver Assistance Techniques & Problem Management 99

Basic instrument monitoring..102

Underwater and surface buoyancy control 103

Controlled Descents and Ascents..106

Out-of-air emergencies 111

Descents lines for Key Scuba Skills...123

Chapter 6: Adaptive Equipment..124

Standard Face mask 126

Prescription/Magnification Mask..127

Full-Face Mask..127

Full-Face Mask with Communications 128

Scuba Fins...128

Webbed gloves..129

Prosthetic Fins...130

Buoyancy Compensation Devices 130

Weighting...131

Wet Suits...132

Dry Suits 132

Transfer Gear & Equipment 133

Protective Matting 134

Belts and Lashes 134

Beach Wheelchairs...134

Underwater Propulsion devices...134

Descent lines with buoy and anchor 135

Regulator Necklace Holder 136

Adaptive Diver Profile Slate 136

Chapter 7: Diveheart's Adaptive Diver Certifications 137

Adaptive Diver and Open Water Certifications 138

Adaptive Diver - Adaptive Dive Team (ADT) 139

Adaptive Diver - Advanced Adaptive Dive Team (AADT) 139

Adaptive Diver - Advanced Adaptive Dive Team Plus special conditions (AADT +) 139

Chapter 8: Imagine the possibilities 141

Environment 144

Research 144

Vision 145

About Diveheart 147

Appendix 149

ACKNOWLEDGMENTS

Diveheart would like to thank the volunteers who gave their time to make this project a success, including: Jeff Myers, Steve Plevin, Jim Hart, Mike Hamel, Jake Freiberger, M.D., Lawrence Dombrowski, Chuck Baldwin, Nikole Ordway, Wilhelmina Stanton, Dan Webb, Tinamarie Hernandez, Betty Carlton, Dr. Ken Sapp, Lisa DePasquale, Kira Heston.

Divers depend on support to do what we do; servicing equipment, filling tanks, providing boats, guiding dive tours…etc. For years D.J. Wood and the professionals at Rainbow Reef in Key Largo Florida have been the "angels" who have watched Diveheart's back as we worked with children, adults and veterans from around the world with the most profound disabilities the dive industry has ever had to cope with.

Not surprisingly D.J. recognized the importance of Diveheart's project to write and produce the most current adaptive training manuals and graciously assigned one of his dive boats and crew to serve as the vessel for many of the training videos and photos you will see throughout this manual. We are honored that D.J.'s Rainbow reef is the first PADI 5 Star Dive Center to recognize and honor Diveheart's Adaptive Diver certification program. Adaptive Divers producing their Diveheart C-card will know that they will be welcomed and a spot on the dive boat will be reserved for them.

It is no secret that Diveheart would not be where it is today without the unselfish generosity, professional support and friendship of D.J. Wood and his incredible team at Rainbow Reef in Key Largo. D.J., Diveheart salutes you and your team for the unwavering friendship and support you have provided over the years, allowing us to move to the next level and help those with disabilities, *"Imagine the Possibilities"* in their lives…thank you.

SPECIAL ACKNOWLEDGMENT

Dear Reader,

I know it will be hard for you to believe that what we are trying to accomplish with this manual and training program is not about scuba diving, but rather about helping children, adults and veterans, not just with disabilities, but of all abilities, to ***Imagine the Possibilities*** in their lives. I had no idea that when I began the process of rethinking how we should present and teach Adaptive Scuba to instructors, dive buddies and individuals with disabilities, that it would take the better part of five years to develop the materials and bring them to market.

No doubt, I had the concept and vision of reinventing adaptive training protocols that would represent the industry's best practices and the latest thinking and techniques in Adaptive Scuba. However, it wasn't until Mike Kaufman came on board as co- author that I really began to see the light at the end of the tunnel.

Mike is a Diveheart board member, Adaptive Scuba Instructor, accomplished attorney in the medical field and all around awesome diver and good friend. He made the commitment to help and it changed everything. Mike committed hundreds of hours of writing, rewriting and conceptualizing new approaches to teaching Adaptive Scuba to the world. His ability to articulate the benefits, protocols, standards and guidelines in this manual represent concepts that have never been expressed before.

Mike created the Needed Scuba Assistance (NSA) protocols and the Adaptive Diver Profile Slate for Adaptive Diver assessments along with the focus on Key Scuba Skills that you will read about in this manual. These tools are unprecedented in Adaptive Scuba training and will make the activity much safer and more enjoyable for the Adaptive Diver, instructor and buddy team.

Mike tapped into his wealth of experience as an Adaptive Scuba Instructor, and extensive legal and medical knowledge to pioneer unprecedented ideas in risk management, safety protocols and Adaptive Scuba training techniques. His approach of consistently placing ownership on the Adaptive Diver regardless of their abilities, helps everyone on the Adaptive Dive Team better understand their roles and responsibilities; before, during and after the dive.

Mike truly gave everything to this project and for that I am eternally grateful, and I could never thank him enough. Our collaboration with Eric Douglas, Ken Berry and Frazier Nivens then brought our concepts and vision to reality. You will witness, as you read these pages, the new standards and best practices in Adaptive Scuba Training that currently exist.

No doubt, it was a process and not an event, but with Mike Kaufman's input, hard work and dedication, the dream became a reality.

Thank you my friend,

Jim Elliott
Founder & President
Diveheart

THE DIVEHEART PROGRAM DEVELOPMENT TEAM

Frazier Nivens – Emmy Award Winning UW Videographer

Frazier Nivens has been in the diving industry most of his life. Today he's now an active teaching status PADI Course Director #4041 living in Key Largo, Florida and has been a PADI member for over 30 years. Frazier managed major diving operations in the Bahamas for Neal Watson's Undersea Adventures and Stuart Cove's diving operation in Nassau, Bahamas. In November of 1990, Frazier started up Nassau Scuba Centre. After leaving the Bahamas in 1999, he moved to Key Largo and was Ocean Divers, a PADI 5 Star Career Development Center's Course Director. He opened his own business, Frazier Nivens, Ocean Imaging Videography Productions specializing in Underwater Videography productions and operating a full editing and post production facility in Key Largo, Florida.

Frazier Nivens is a National Association of Television Arts and Sciences Emmy Award Winning Film Maker, for excellence in programming, Sharks, Killer's of the Caribbean". Frazier was selected as a Silver Council Telly Award Judge for 2009 & 2010.

Ken Berry – Video Director/ Editor

Ken has worked as a Producer/Director/ Cameraman in the video production business for over 25 years. The early years included gigs for ESPN surfing tournaments, a feature film, commercials, corporate marketing and training, real estate, travel and music videos.

The last 20 of those years have primarily been in the scuba diving industry. His career at PADI – the

Professional Association of Diving Instructors began as their in-house Producer/Director. Eventually, as PADI Executive Producer, he became a key player in converting DSAT – Diving Science and Technology, into PADI in-house media production department. Ken eventually moved on to DAN – Divers Alert Network after receiving an offer to start their in-house media production department. He left DAN in October 2009 and created Living Water Media, a full-service media production company. In those roles, Berry has likely created more scuba training and marketing motion media material than anyone in recreational scuba diving.

Eric Douglas – Editor/Educational Design

Eric Douglas worked for PADI/DSAT from 1998 to 2000 acting as a technical writer and Assistant Editor of The Undersea Journal. He became a Diver Medical Technician in California as well. In 2000, he moved to North Carolina to take over the Training and Education Department at Divers Alert Network. While at DAN, Eric developed or revised every training program offered by DAN, writing video scripts, student materials and instructor manuals. He also designed and developed on online training platform for DAN and traveled internationally teaching the other DAN offices to use the software. Eric has issued more than 1500 DAN certifications, at every level from provider to instructor to trainer and has also taught classes in how use hyperbaric chambers and DMT courses.

Eric has also written a series of dive adventure novels, short stories and children's books. He co-authored the book Scuba Diving Safety with Dan Orr and is currently the Lessons for Life columnist for Scuba Diving Magazine.

Michael Kaufman – Adaptive Scuba Instructor

Michael Roy Kaufman is a veteran trial attorney and practicing in the South Florida area for the past 34 years, receiving his Juris Doctorate in 1980, and his MBA in 1976. His legal career has exclusively dealt with representing individuals suffering disabilities and families who have suffered a loss as a result of the wrongful conduct of others.

For the past 48 years, Mike Kaufman has been an active diver whose passion and love for the aquatic world has driven him to extensively explore the coral reef systems of Florida and throughout the world. He is a PADI instructor; Diveheart Adaptive Scuba Instructor; Handicapped Scuba Association (HSA) instructor, EFR instructor and a USCG licensed captain. In 2007, he was inspired by the great work of Diveheart; and felt it was time for him to combine his underwater passions with his interest to serve individuals with disabilities.

Among other contributions, Mike and Diveheart's President, Jim Elliot, collaborated to create new and improved protocols, guidelines, and standards for adaptive scuba training. He is a Diveheart Ambassador serving the South Florida region, and, currently serves on Diveheart's Board of Directors. Mike is also a co-founding member of DiveBar, a bar association composed of legal professionals that promotes education and awareness about coral reefs and the marine environment through scuba diving and philanthropic activities.

Jim Elliott – Adaptive Scuba Instructor and Trainer

After a 30 year career in the media business, including years at the Chicago Tribune, WGN Radio and CLTV News, Jim Elliott began training divers with disabilities full time. First, in 1997, as a PADI instructor, then progressing to instructor trainer in 2004 with the Handicapped Scuba Association and then Scuba Diving International.

He founded the nonprofit Diveheart in 2001 and has lead the way in helping to pioneer adaptive scuba training, research, rehabilitation, education and promotion around the world. In addition to almost two hundred cities throughout the U.S., this also includes China, Australia, Israel, the UK, and all over the Caribbean. Jim is a Divers Alert Network and Medic First Aid instructor. He's won local, national and international awards for volunteerism and humanitarianism and he's co-authored two books. Jim has been featured on CNN, NBC, ABC, CBS, PBS, Money Magazine, Huffington Post, Chicago Tribune, Miami Herald, San Diego Tribune and numerous other publications and media outlets worldwide. More recently, Jim has presented to hyperbaric and medical conferences around the country about Diveheart and scuba therapy. Jim is a Rotarian in Downers Grove Illinois and works with Rotary around the world to serve others while starting new programs.

As part of Diveheart, Jim launched Diveheart Military Wounded to serve veterans with disabilities. This has won Diveheart grants from the Department of Veterans affairs, AMVETS and others. Through DMW, Jim has facilitated adaptive scuba programs with Navy Seals in Coronado, Marines at Camp Pendleton, as well as initiating programs at Fort Lewis, McCoy, Knox, Great Lakes Naval Base and V.A. Hospitals and others around the country.

CHAPTER 1: INTRODUCTION

Congratulations, on deciding to join a select number of people in the world: Scuba Divers!

This decision will change your life in ways you may not even imagine. By the time you finish your last open water certification dive, you will better understand Diveheart's mantra...

"Imagine the Possibilities"

Not only will you be a member of an elite and privileged community who can explore, enjoy and experience the beautiful and exciting underwater world, you will be empowered with a new and enhanced sense of your own capacities. No longer will you view your disability as an impediment to things you may want to do, but rather you will adapt and pursue any endeavor with a "can do" attitude. You are about to embark on a journey filled with fun, adventure and immeasurable rewards.

Philosophy, Program Description and Goals

Diveheart believes anybody can be a scuba diver, regardless of their *abilities* (with just a few exceptions) and that adaptive scuba training should be no different than what others receive through nationally recognized scuba training agencies. In addition, Diveheart's Adaptive Scuba Training Program provides supplemental instruction, guidelines and protocols regarding the three main features of Adaptive Scuba:

1. Use of special modifications and techniques enabling performance of scuba skills
2. Enhancement of the "buddy system"(the adaptive dive team approach to safely enjoying scuba), by requiring two specially-trained buddy divers to assist in the performance of required scuba skills; and
3. Using Adaptive Scuba equipment

Your Diveheart Adaptive Scuba Instructor has specialized knowledge, training and experience to teach scuba to individuals with all types of abilities, including quadriplegics, paraplegics, various neuromuscular disorders, amputees, blindness, deafness, etc. Their training and experience qualifies them to assess your special needs for assistance with scuba-related activities and how to address those needs. Of even greater importance, your instructor will teach you how to perform your own "Scuba Needs" assessments to identify the degree to which you may require assistance and how to use modified techniques to address those needs—this will empower you to become a safe and competent diver.

Based on those assessments your Adaptive Scuba Instructor will determine what type of qualified buddy divers should be on your dive team and what type of scuba certification you will be eligible to receive. In short, Diveheart's philosophy is to partner-up dive teams where each member, including the Adaptive Diver, is specially trained and experienced to coordinate and render assistance to each other.

Your instructor will provide you with the course materials of a nationally recognized scuba training agency. Those materials will teach you basic diving knowledge, scuba skills needed to dive safely, and the importance of the buddy system. Additionally, with this manual and your instructor's experience

and training, you will work together to modify and make adaptations so you can perform scuba skills independently, to the extent possible.

If you are not able to perform all the required scuba skills independently, your Diveheart Adaptive Scuba Instructor will teach you how to perform those same skills with the assistance of specially-trained Adaptive Dive Buddies or Adaptive Scuba Instructors. You will also learn how adaptive scuba gear can give you the capacity to perform scuba skills which may otherwise be difficult for you to do.

Diveheart's training program is unique in that it gives individuals with disabilities an opportunity to earn two open water certifications. One certification is from a nationally-recognized scuba training agency. You can earn that certification if, after training and practice, you are able to modify techniques to perform all the required scuba skills independently. You can also earn Diveheart's Adaptive Diver certification.

For those divers with disabilities who qualify for both certifications an additional benefit is conferred. In case such diver's disabilities progress to a point where they can no longer perform necessary scuba skills independently, they will still have an opportunity to dive by using their Diveheart certification card.

Most importantly, and regardless of whether you earn one or two certifications, you will have the supplemental knowledge and experience of Diveheart's training—a program specifically designed to give Adaptive Divers the tools they need for safe diving.

CHAPTER 2: DIVEHEART'S ADAPTIVE DIVE TEAM APPROACH AND YOUR RESPONSIBILITY TO SHARE INFORMATION

For your safety, and the safety of your Adaptive Dive team, you must be willing to share information including your medical history. If you haven't already done so, you will be required to sign a Health Insurance Portability and Accountability Act (HIPAA) waiver form prior to training so Diveheart may share pertinent medical information with your Adaptive Scuba Instructor and others that may be involved in your training. You will also be required to fill out Diveheart's Adaptive Diver Registry form which is designed to obtain important information about you, so your instructor and Adaptive Dive Team can give you the training and assistance you need. The goal is to build a relationship where you are comfortable working with instructors and Adaptive Dive Team members who understand important information about you and your team, and your instructors are comfortable working with you.

It is *your responsibility* to provide an accurate medical history and a frank and honest assessment of your special needs and the scope of your abilities. Your Adaptive Dive Team will use that information to address, modify and adapt your scuba training to your individual needs.

Your instructor and Adaptive Dive Team will begin learning about you and how to work with your special scuba needs as soon as they meet you. If you have limited mobility and are ambulatory, but still may need a wheelchair in certain circumstances, your team will err on the side of caution and will assume you may need a higher level of assistance than you truly require. Your candid communication with your team (for example, how you like to transfer or do other tasks) will help them immensely while they assist you during your dive training.

Diveheart believes in the "Challenge by Choice" philosophy. Your Diveheart team will encourage you to attempt all scuba skills and will make necessary adaptations so you can achieve a comfort level acceptable to you, and will always respect your assessment on how or whether you feel capable of performing any particular skill. You and your Diveheart Adaptive Dive Team will work together to help you meet the challenge to become a certified diver.

This same philosophy applies to your Adaptive Dive Team. If you are not comfortable working with a particular Adaptive Dive Buddy or Adaptive Scuba Instructor, or you do not wish to attempt a certain skill with one of your dive buddies, it is completely acceptable to make the necessary changes to your team or simply not attempt the skill. The same guidelines apply to your team members. Diveheart training is a process, not an event, and the most important process in play is how the team works and assists each other.

At the core of Diveheart's training protocol is the requirement that all members of the dive team, including the Adaptive Diver, know how to assess a diver's special needs for scuba assistance and how to meet those needs thru the application of modified techniques and equipment. In the next chapter you will be introduced to Diveheart's method for performing an assessment—it's called the (NSA) Needed Scuba Assistance evaluation. A tool that you and your team can use for all of your diving experiences, making your dive planning and trips more organized, fun and enjoyable.

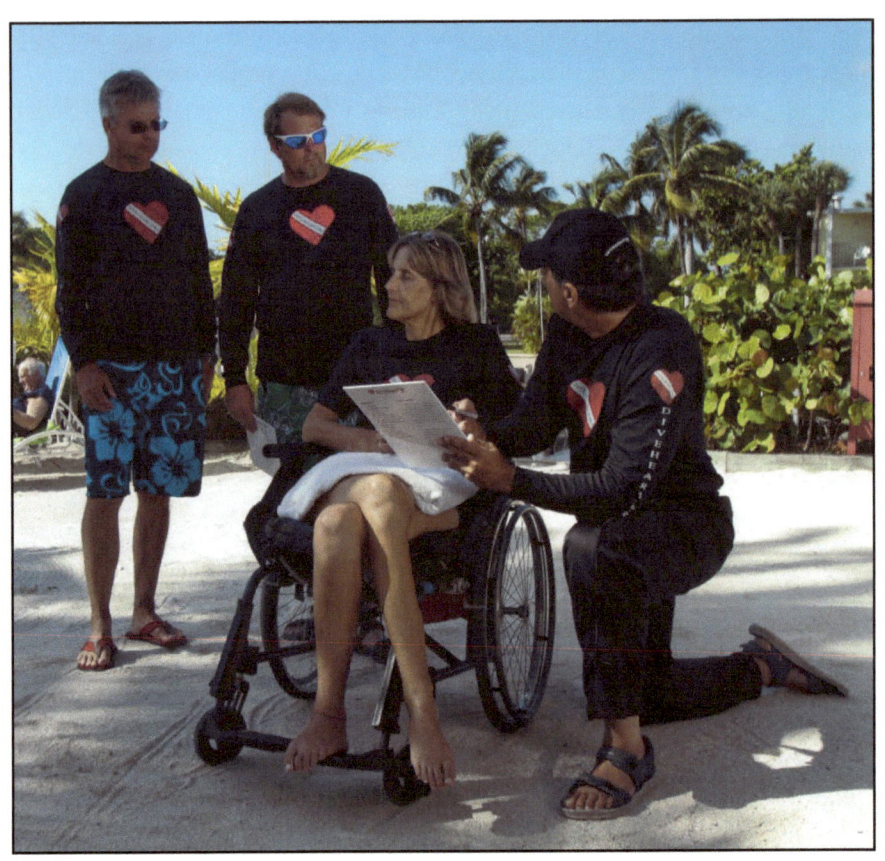

CHAPTER 3: NEEDED SCUBA ASSISTANCE (NSA) EVALUATION:

Throughout your training, you and your Diveheart Adaptive Scuba Instructor will assess your ability to perform the required scuba skills, with or without assistance, and whether you will require any special scuba equipment.

Diveheart's <u>N</u>eeded <u>S</u>cuba <u>A</u>ssistance (NSA) evaluation is an assessment tool that focuses on whether you can independently perform, with or without modifications, the 20 scuba skills required for open water certification or whether you require assistance.

The NSA evaluation is an ongoing process starting with your own initial assessment using the "Adaptive Diver NSA Self Assessment" form. You will find a copy of the form in the Appendix along with instruction on how to complete it. Your instructor will be available to answer any questions you may have. As you will see, the form simply asks you to self assess whether you think you may need assistance with any of the basic scuba skills in view of your abilities. It is a very preliminary self assessment to give your instructor a sense of what you believe your capacity to perform the scuba skills is after you have learned how the skills are performed. In consideration of your self assessment and at an early point in the program your Diveheart Adaptive Scuba Instructor will also perform an initial NSA evaluation. To the extent that you cannot initially perform the skills independently, your instructor will help you use adaptive methods and equipment so you can perform them on your own. If that is not possible, you will work with your Adaptive Scuba Instructor so you can effectively execute the skill.

It's all about team work.

Example: A diver who cannot reach and recover his regulator if it falls from his mouth because of a right arm amputation may be able to perform the regulator recovery skill by modifying his equipment. The regulator hose can be switched to the left side.

The NSA evaluation is the foundation to Diveheart's integrated Adaptive Training Program. The NSA system not only serves to identify the nature and extent of your special scuba needs, but also determines the qualifications of your Adaptive Dive Team, as well as your eligibility for the different types of Adaptive Scuba Certifications issued by Diveheart.

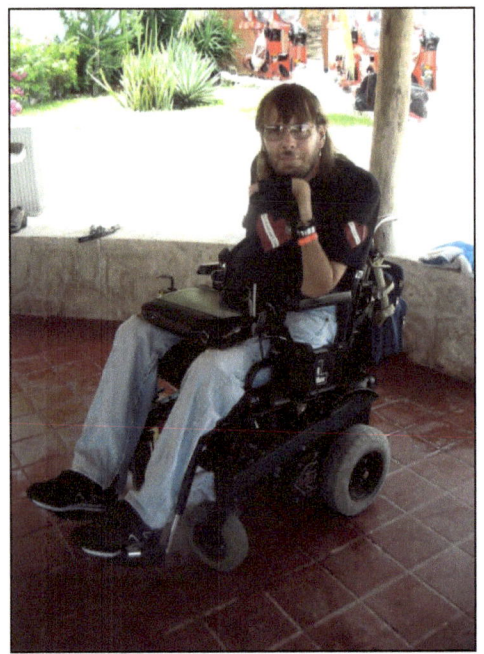

If you can successfully perform all required scuba skills independently, with or without modifications or adaptive gear, you will be eligible for both the nationally recognized open water certification and Diveheart's Adaptive Diver certification.

If you need special assistance from another diver to perform required scuba skills, then you will be required to dive with an Adaptive Dive Team consisting of two certified Adaptive Dive Buddies and your certification will be conditioned on diving with them.

Similarly, if the NSA evaluation indicates you need a greater level of assistance or assistance with certain *key* scuba skills, you will be required to have a certified Adaptive Dive Buddy and an Advanced Adaptive Dive Buddy or an Adaptive Scuba Instructor on your team. Your scuba certification will indicate the makeup of your Adaptive Dive Team.

An Emphasis on Key Scuba Skills for Safety

The NSA evaluation will highlight whether you require assistance to perform the following scuba skills or may need the following adaptive equipment:

- Controlled ascents and descents
- Equalization of ears and mask
- Out-of-air emergency alternatives (i.e. share air, buddy breathe, etc.)

- Use of a Full-Face Mask or other special equipment required for underwater breathing.

These skills are particularly important to perform correctly in order to dive safely. You must perform controlled ascents and descents and ear and mask equalization to reduce the risk of injury from barotrauma such as:
- mask squeeze
- ear drum rupture
- lung overexpansion injuries
- arterial gas embolism
- decompression sickness

Similarly, out-of-air emergencies must be managed timely and coordinated effectively with your dive team to avert the associated risk of these events.

Since these particular skills require greater communications, coordination and synchronization between you and your dive team, Diveheart advocates the practice of assembling a more experienced dive team to assist adaptive divers who require assistance with key scuba skills—a practice that will enhance dive safety for everyone.

Diveheart's NSA system is all about creating the greatest margin of safety and fun for the entire adaptive dive team.

Ongoing Evaluation and the Final NSA Course Evaluation

Throughout your training, you and your Diveheart Adaptive Scuba Instructor will continuously re-evaluate your capacity to execute the required scuba skills. You may always require assistance with some skills and others you may be able to perform independently with hard work and practice using modified techniques or adaptive equipment.

After you have successfully completed all course requirements, your Diveheart Adaptive Scuba Instructor will perform a final NSA evaluation to determine your certification eligibility and the qualifications of your adaptive dive team.

Self-NSA Assessments Post Certification—Your Continuing Responsibility

After you receive your Open Water and/or Diveheart Adaptive Diver certifications, and embark upon the fun-filled journey of exploring the underwater world, you will have a continuing responsibility to evaluate your fitness and capacity to perform scuba skills with and without assistance. Your ability may change with time and you are best qualified to assess that change by using the NSA self assessment form.

If your certification requires that you dive with Adaptive Dive Buddies, it is your responsibility to review with them everything they need to know about your abilities to assist you with having a safe and enjoyable dive. This information should include all the scuba skills that you need assistance with, how you perform those skills with assistance, and any adaptive gear you may use.

Diveheart's Post Certification NSA Commitment

At any time after you receive your Diveheart Adaptive Diver certification, you believe you require more or less assistance with required scuba skills, you may schedule an appointment with a Diveheart Adaptive Scuba Instructor to update your NSA evaluation for recertification with appropriate conditions, if any, based upon the level of scuba assistance required.

Creating an Adaptive Diver's Profile

The NSA evaluation creates a specific and personalized profile that identifies vital information about you and your special needs for assistance with scuba diving. It is information YOU must convey to your Adaptive Dive Team.

A meaningful Adaptive Diver's Profile should include the following basic information about you:

- Name and age
- Sizing info for scuba gear
- Relevant medical history (e.g. spinal cord injury T-4)
- NSA score
- Type of Adaptive Dive Certification
- Names of Adaptive Team members
- Your impairments affecting performance of scuba skills (i.e. mobility, sensory, thermal, hearing, visual)
- Your needs for assistance with basics scuba skills
- Your needs for assistance with Key scuba skills (i.e. out of air emergencies, controlled descents/ascents, and equalization)
- Your need for Full Face Mask equipment
- Your need for Adaptive equipment
- Special precautions that need to be observed (i.e. autonomic dysreflexia, pressure sores, etc.)
- Other info that is relevant to provide reasonable assistance necessary to enhance safety and diving enjoyment

Your adaptive diver profile may turn out to be as dynamic as your personality and may change over time. This is why you must perform updated assessments whenever you perceive a change in your abilities so you and your dive team can make any adjustment to your requirements for special assistance.

To aid you in remembering all of your special scuba needs Diveheart created the Adaptive Diver Profile Slate (ADPS). In another section of this manual you will learn that the ADPS is a very useful tool in planning your diving adventures and PREDIVE BRIEFINGS.

CHAPTER 4: ENHANCED BUDDY SYSTEM—*THE ADAPTIVE DIVE TEAM*

Teaming up with another scuba diver and staying close to each other during the dive to provide assistance and support is known as the "Buddy System" and should be followed by all divers regardless of their abilities. Your buddy team not only makes diving safer but is a practical way to dive and adds to the enjoyment that comes with sharing a fun and adventurous experience.

From a safety and practicality standpoint, your dive buddy team assists you with a variety of scuba-related skills, including all required scuba skills, predive planning, safety checks and underwater emergencies, entanglements, loose scuba gear or other problems, both major and minor.

Diveheart's Adaptive Scuba program enhances the level of assistance offered by the buddy system in two significant ways:

(1) By requiring a three man adaptive dive team consisting of you and two certified Adaptive Dive Buddies and/or Adaptive Scuba Instructors; and,

(2) By requiring you to conduct a predive briefing with your team that covers all the information that comprises your unique Adaptive Diver's Profile (i.e. vital info regarding you and your special scuba needs).

Adaptive Diver's Responsibility to Communicate Special Modifications and Needed Assistance.

Regardless of your impairments or abilities, it is always your responsibility to know how to perform all scuba skills either independently, with or without modification, or with or without assistance from your Adaptive Dive Buddies. The primary objective of this training program is for YOU to first recognize which scuba skills may require modifications or assistance and then learn adaptive techniques that will enable you to perform them. After your training, YOU are responsible for communicating with your Adaptive Dive Team specifically how to do those skills, who will provide assistance, and how the team will coordinate that assistance.

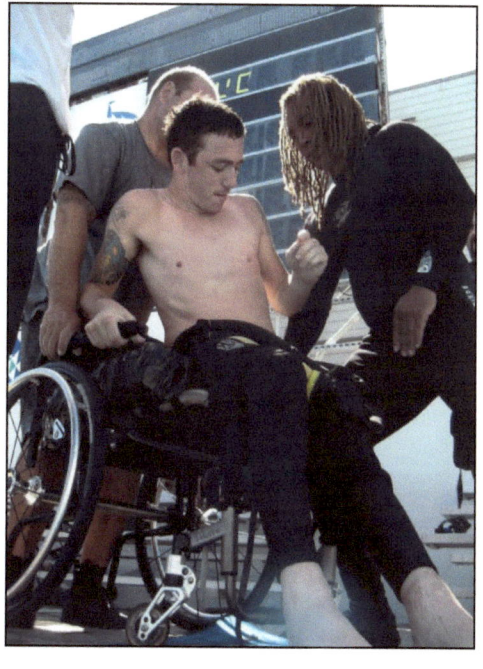

You should communicate that information well in advance of the proposed dive and ALWAYS during the predive briefing. That will help avoid confusion as to who is doing what, when and where. Consequently, the planned dive will be safer and more enjoyable.

For example, if you have a sensory impairment and are at risk for developing a pressure sore if you don't use padded cushions, you need to tell your team about your condition and request the necessary assistance. You should review with the team the need to have the cushion available for all transfers, including those made for positioning on the deck for donning wetsuits and to the dive platform. You will also need to review how the team should coordinate transfers and equipment movements by requesting *specific assistance from specific members of the team. This should include who will help you transfer from the chair to the dive platform, who will take the seat cushion from the wheelchair and move it to the dive platform. The briefing should also include how the pad should be moved back to the dive platform prior to the team transferring you from the water back onto the platform, and then again from the platform back to the wheelchair. You must walk through the logistics of this process carefully during the pre-dive briefing so everyone on the team is clear as to their roles and assignments.*

This example underscores the general approach to communicating with your team for all scuba skills and related activities that may require assistance. Never assume that your Adaptive Dive Team will know how to best provide assistance unless you meet your responsibility to communicate.

Also, as an integral member of the dive team, it is your responsibility to only dive with appropriately qualified Adaptive Dive Buddies as noted on your Adaptive Diver certification card. It is your responsibility to request the certification cards of anybody serving as a member of your dive team to verify that they have the appropriate adaptive certification.

Your responsibility includes notifying everyone involved in the dive, from other divers to the dive shop and dive boat crew, that you are required to dive with certified Adaptive Dive Buddies as noted on your certification card.

Diveheart's Adaptive Dive Team approach is a benefit to all members of the team adding redundancy in safety, practicality, and perhaps just as important, more fun and enjoyment that comes with sharing exciting diving experiences with others.

The Roles of Your Adaptive Dive Buddies

The primary role of the Adaptive Dive Buddy is to provide you assistance with required scuba skills, procedures, equipment and taking special precautions. Your team can only fulfill that role if you inform each member of the team of your adaptive diver profile. Among other information, your profile generally includes:

- the nature and extent of your impairments
- special precautions that you must observe due to your medical condition
- which scuba skills or procedures you may, or do, need help with
- any special scuba gear or other equipment you may need

Review your Adaptive Diver Profile Slate with your team. It will help guide your discussions in an orderly and methodical way so that each team member will know their role.

Primary and Secondary Roles of the Adaptive Dive Team

The diver with the highest level of certification or experience should serve as the leader of the dive team. Given time and experience, that may ultimately be you. Naturally, during your training, your Adaptive Scuba Instructor will always be your team leader. You will work with the team leader to decide and agree upon who will do what. If you need assistance with controlled ascents and descents, equalization, out of air emergency alternatives, or need a Full-Face Mask, the team leader will determine how and who will provide assistance—with your approval.

Example: if a double arm amputee needs assistance removing gear at the surface for transfer out of the water, the team leader may decide who will inflate the BCD at the surface and release all straps and buckles for removal of equipment and who will secure the gear and deliver it to the boat crew.

Predive Briefings with the Adaptive Dive Team

One of the most important protocols of Adaptive Diving is the Predive Briefing. The predive briefing includes all members of your dive team and takes place before you arrive at the dive site. It is important for you to discuss and review all relevant information and procedures, and how the team will coordinate their efforts from the moment you begin gearing up to the moment you return to the poolside, shoreline or dive boat. You and the dive team leader are responsible for directing the conversation and making sure everyone agrees.

A good and effective briefing must include the following:

Review with the team any *conditions* you have on your Adaptive Diver Certification Card.

If you require assistance with controlled descents you must dive with one certified Advanced Adaptive Dive Buddy (or higher) and one certified Adaptive Dive Buddy.

Review relevant medical conditions that relate to your abilities, medical aids and devices you use, and the list of scuba skills that require assistance and how to render assistance.

You tell your team "I suffered a military wound resulting in loss of my fingers. I need assistance with ear equalization because I can't pinch the nose piece on my mask. I generally need to descend slowly and equalize frequently. I also need assistance with mask clearing."

Review which team members will have primary responsibility to provide assistance with which scuba skills.

You need help managing ascents and descents and mask clearing. You will discuss with the team leader who will be managing the inflation/deflation of your BCD and how you will clear your mask.

Review with the team leader who, when, where and how transfers on and off the dive boat and in and out of the water will take place.

Who will transfer the paralyzed Adaptive Diver to dive platform; who will move dive gear to the platform; who will assist the Adaptive Diver with donning scuba equipment?

Review any special hand signals and other methods for communicating underwater.

Due to partial paralysis of a hand, you review how you have modified the "OK" hand signal.

Review and confirm that all adaptive dive gear is available and ready for the dive.

If you need a Full-Face Mask and a transfer harness, you will let your team know and make sure the equipment is available for the dive.

Review with the team leader any weather, boating or underwater environmental conditions (such as currents) which may affect your ability to dive safely and plan accordingly.

Due to moderate currents, decide who will give you assistance with underwater and surface swimming if you weaken before the end of the dive.

Review with the team any special precautions that should be observed in view of your medical impairments.

A diver who has sensory impairment below his waist and needs to protect against pressure sores should advise his team and make sure that a protective pad is available.

Since there is a considerable amount of information to review during the predive briefing, you and your Adaptive Dive Team should use the Adaptive Diver Profile Slate for every dive as a checklist to help organize and guide the briefing and to ensure that everything is covered. This is similar to the commercial airline pilot who is required to use a checklist each and every time he flies regardless of his experience or seniority.

At the conclusion of the briefing, the last question is: **Are you comfortable and in total agreement with the dive plan as discussed during the briefing?**

If the answer is no, or you do not agree with any aspect of the dive plan, then further discussion must occur until there is complete agreement among the entire dive team. In the unlikely event that all parties are not in complete agreement, the matter must be reviewed by the event leader to decide how to best proceed with the dive.

Use Diveheart's Adaptive Diver Profile Slate during your predive briefing. It is there to remind you of everything you are responsible to review with your adaptive dive team.

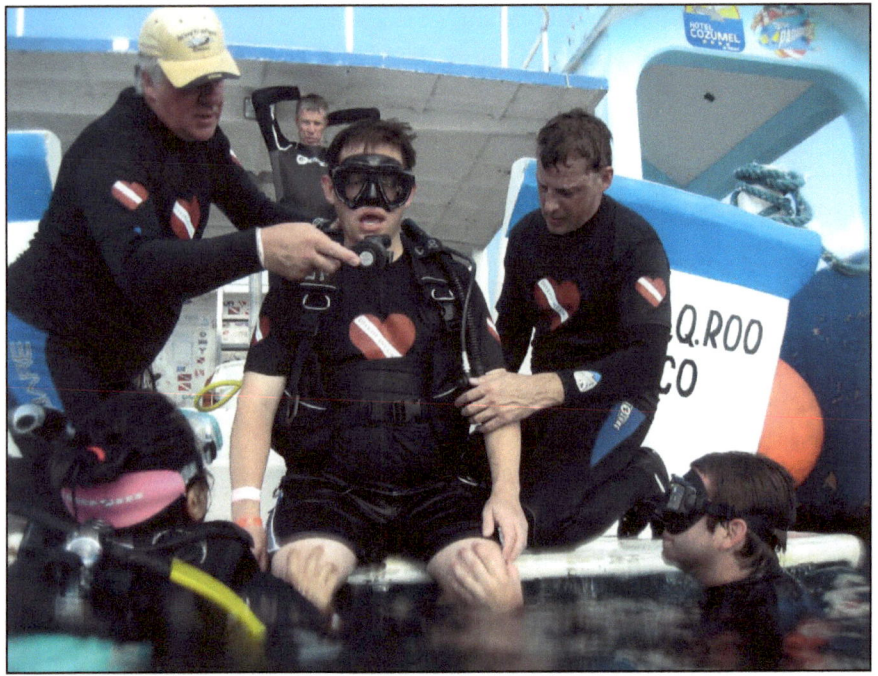

CHAPTER 5: LEARNING ADAPTIVE DIVING

As an Adaptive Scuba student, you learn the same material and perform the same required scuba skills that are outlined in the open water scuba certification course. Your Diveheart Adaptive Scuba Instructor will provide all the necessary instructions and tutoring you will need to make sure you understand all the required principles related to scuba diving so you may dive safely and have fun. Additionally, your instructor will provide supplemental information and training regarding adaptive diving protocols, guidelines and special Diveheart standards that will give you the best opportunity to enjoy the exciting sport of scuba with specially-trained divers that share your excitement to dive.

Independent study program

The academic portion of most scuba courses is accomplished using independent study techniques. This allows you to learn and review the material at your own pace. Typically, you will need to independently study those materials and Diveheart's supplemental adaptive training manual prior to attending the pool sessions to begin in-water training. Each scuba training agency is a bit different so you will need to discuss this portion of the program with your instructor. Most instructors briefly review the academic material at the pool before getting students in the water.

If you are uncomfortable with this learning style or your disability makes this difficult, discuss learning options with your instructor.

Performing Scuba Skills with Adaptations

"Improvise, adapt, overcome and conquer"
The mantra of the US Marine Corp also embodies the spirit of Diveheart.

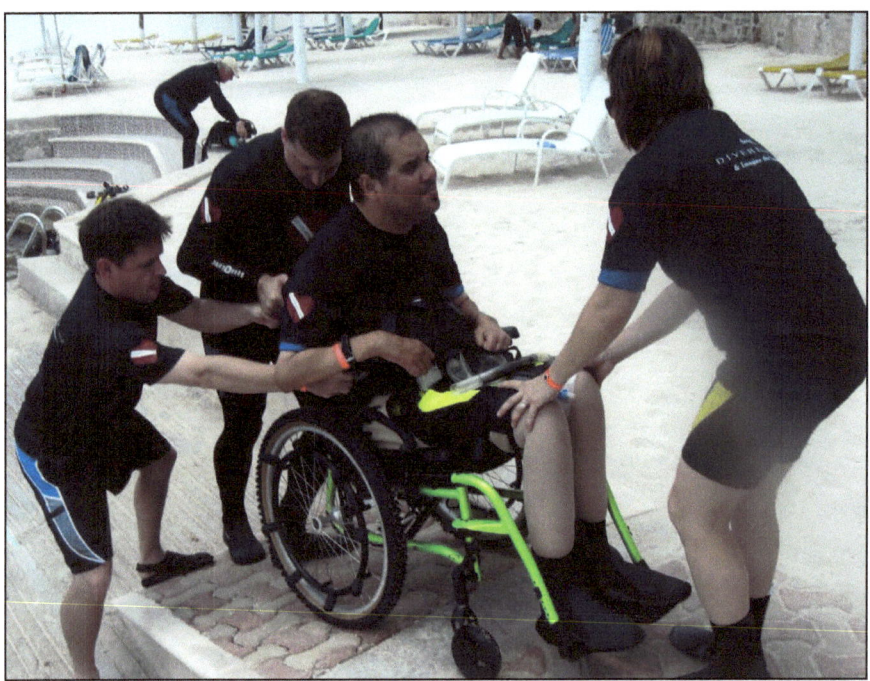

Your Diveheart Adaptive Scuba Instructor has been trained to implement a wide variety of possible adaptations, modifications, special equipment and gear to help you accomplish each of the required scuba skills so you can learn to dive safely as an Adaptive Diver.

The typical process for a class is the instructor will explain how to perform scuba skills and present real-time demonstrations. Afterwards, you and your instructor will discuss the skills and make an assessment concerning your abilities to perform them in view of your impairments as discussed in Chapter 3. You and your instructor will perform an NSA evaluation to facilitate that assessment. Once accomplished, your instructor will provide training on how to use adaptive techniques, procedures, equipment and team work which may help you execute all scuba skills depending upon your specific needs and impairments.

Special Adaptations, Techniques, Procedures and Team Work—for the Performance of Scuba Skills

In the remainder of this chapter, you will learn how to modify scuba skills in view of the different types of physical and/or sensory impairments you may have. The guidelines, protocols and procedures described here are based upon the best practices used by Diveheart Adaptive Scuba Instructors for a wide range of disabilities that primarily consider upper/lower mobility impairments, sensory impairments, including tactile, thermal, visual, and, hearing, as well as, other special needs and precautions.

There are no specific standards on how to modify the techniques used to perform scuba skills; it's really a matter of figuring out what works best considering your unique set of abilities. However, what is presented here will serve as a good basis for you and your Adaptive Dive Team to formulate special modifications enabling you to perform skills independently or to develop procedures for how your Adaptive Dive Buddies can best assist you.

Although, these practices, procedures, guidelines, etc., are described generally, they may not always be appropriate for you given your unique set of abilities. You and your instructor may need to get creative, improvise and find new ways to enable you to properly perform scuba skills. Therefore, if any specific modification or technique described below proves to be ineffective, or unsafe, then you and your instructor must make the necessary changes.

The goal is to become proficient and safe in performing all scuba skills with or without assistance.

Once you have learned how to perform each of the required scuba skills, you need to remember which ones "did" require, or "may" require assistance, and how you specifically used modified techniques to perform them, including how each member of the dive team provided assistance. During your training, take notes on each scuba skill where you needed assistance. Throughout your training, and after successful certification, you will need to review that information with your dive team during pre-dive briefings. Refer to your notes until you feel comfortable remembering how to explain to your dive team how, who, what, when and where you will need assistance.

In addition to information on special techniques and modified practices, the next section will highlight some special precautions you should observe due to certain medical conditions or impairments you may have and which your dive team must know about.

For example, a diver with thermal regulation impairments needs to exercise precautions to protect against hot or cold environments. You will also learn what you need to review at Pre-Dive Briefings so your dive team can be prepared to assist you with special precautions.

Once you have learned how to perform scuba skills using adaptive techniques, it is important to practice these skills from time to time so you do not become stale in knowledge or execution. Also, with practice you may

discover new ways to adapt to your impairments and become more independent in skill performance.

Learning to perfect adaptations is a good way to empower your senses with a "Can Do" attitude and become all that you can be—an attitude that will transcend your scuba diving experiences and bring positive changes to your life.

IMAGINE the POSSIBILITIES!!!

Improvise, Adapt, Overcome and Conquer Scuba Skills

After your instructor demonstrates each scuba skill, discuss how you believe any impairment may affect your ability to perform the skill and make an assessment how assistance can enable you to successfully execute them. Together, you and your instructor will work out how to complete the skill with adaptations, assistance, or using special equipment. This applies to all the skills you will be trained to execute.

Each section relates to a scuba skill and will provide information how to perform the skill in consideration of (5) five types of physical impairments:

1. Mobility impairments
2. Visual Impairments
3. Hearing Impairments
4. Sensory Impairments
5. Thermal Impairments

You may have one, some, or all of these impairments. The severity of each type may vary from mild to severe, and may differ from day to day. Some of your limbs may function differently from the other. The vision in one eye can be vastly different from the other, as can your hearing. Any dysfunction due to paralysis, spasticity, weakness, restricted motion may also fall within a wide spectrum from mild to severe. Sensory and thermal impairments are also variable depending on all sorts of factors. Your impairments may be stable or getting progressively better or worse over time.

Because of human variability it is impossible to write a training manual that would address your specific and unique set of abilities. However the following section will provide you with meaningful information, strategies, protocols, best practices and standards that will help you and your Adaptive Dive Team address your special needs.

Diveheart encourages you to read the entire section for each type of impairment, pay particular attention to the impairments that apply to you.

Diving system assembly and disassembly

Visual Impairments

If you have visual impairments, it is still possible for you to assemble your gear, but you will need to be patient and diligent in practicing this skill. Begin with getting acquainted "tactilely" with your equipment. Globally feel your equipment and then focus on each individual component and how it fits into the completed assembly. Your instructor will describe what you are touching, how to assemble the gear, and decide to what extent you may need assistance from others. Although assistance may be required at first, practice the skill with the intent of eliminating the need for assistance, if possible.

It is especially important for the Visually-impaired diver to be able to describe his equipment by make, model, color or other distinguishing features. This will greatly assist your Adaptive Dive Buddies with locating your gear for assembly and disassembly. It is also a good idea to specially tag the equipment with discernible tactile clues so the Visually-impaired diver can identify his own gear.

Mobility Impairments

Regardless of any physical impairment you may have (one arm amputee, paralysis of arms and legs, etc.) it is always your responsibility to know how to assemble and disassemble your scuba equipment. The Adaptive Dive Buddy team is there to provide assistance to the extent you need it.

Guidelines for Assembly of Full-Face Mask

For those Adaptive Divers who require a Full-Face Mask, the same is true—the Adaptive Diver must confirm proper assembly, with or without assistance from the Adaptive Dive Team before the dive. It is essential to review the operating or instructional manual for the brand and model of the mask before using it. Most manufacturers' websites have links to their owner manuals for each unit they produce that specifically sets forth how they should be assembled. DO NOT USE A FULL-FACE MASK UNLESS YOU UNDERSTAND and have confirmed that at least one member of your dive team understands, the proper assembly, use and operation of the mask.

Generally, you should confirm proper Full-Face Mask assembly which includes:

- Attachment of Full-Face Mask hose to low pressure port of regulator first stage
- Attachment of alternate air source (octopus regulator)
- Attachment of bailout mask to a BCD D ring or other appropriate attachment
- Confirmation of battery insertion, if communication device is used

- Testing of audio function if communication device is required and verifying proper assembly of companion unit.
- Attachment of redundant air supply valve and assembly with pony tank for divers who cannot perform an emergency bailout

Assembly Considerations for Thermally-Impaired divers

For Adaptive Divers who have thermal regulation dysfunction, it's important to make sure you have assembled and have available appropriate clothing and necessary warming or cooling tools ready for use.

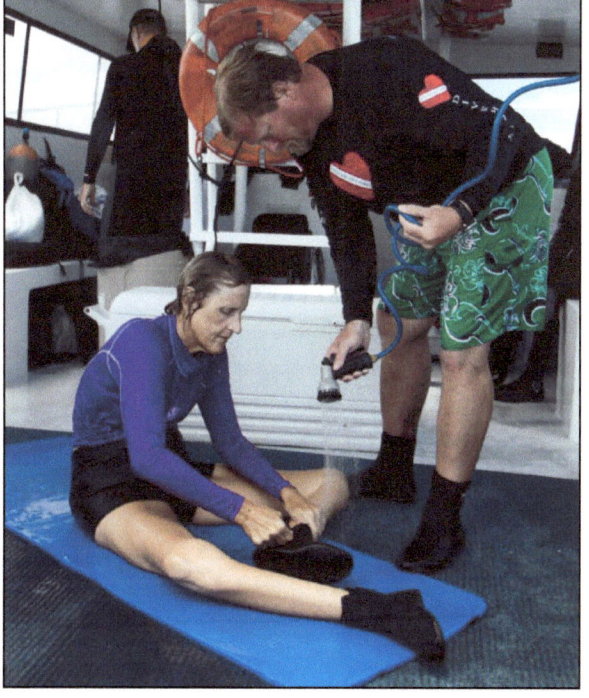

If overheating is a foreseeable concern, check for:

- Dockside and dive boat water hoses for cool down rinses or cool water buckets
- Cooling fans or misters
- Wet rags
- Ice supply
- Broad rim sun shielding hats
- Sufficient water on boat for hydration purposes

If hypothermic conditions are foreseeable, prepare to have some or all of the following accommodations:

- Dockside or dive boat warm water hoses for warming
- Extra clothing apparel- thermal lined wind breakers, etc.
- Chemical warming packs
- Wetsuits of appropriate thickness for the conditions

- Topside hoods and wetsuit hoods
- Dry suits for properly trained Adaptive Divers
- Donning and removing scuba equipment and apparel topside

Dive gear assembly naturally includes having all of the equipment present and available. The Adaptive Diver should prepare and review an equipment check list which includes all special gear for adaptive use. The Adaptive Diver Profile Slate has a section itemizing commonly used adaptive equipment which you should review to confirm all special equipment is present.

As you might suspect, your responsibility to disassemble your equipment is no different, and to make sure that you have reviewed your dive equipment check list and have re-packed all of your gear. Remember if you need assistance your Adaptive Dive Team is there to lend a helping hand—simply ask, but do not assume they will take over your responsibilities.

Equipment inspection (at water's edge)

Regardless of the extent of your impairments, it is always your responsibility to inspect your scuba equipment or request assistance from your Adaptive Dive Buddy team. Any oversight during the equipment inspection process may result in significant problems. It's like packing your own parachute for sky diving.

It is critically important that you conduct, oversee or supervise the equipment inspection process. You must personally observe, or otherwise personally confirm that all scuba equipment is functional and operational. This means you must also perform your own pre-dive safety checks. Asking one or more Adaptive Dive Team members to perform a pre-dive safety check of your equipment outside of your presence or without your ability to personally confirm that it has been done, is wrong and contrary to your responsibilities. The team is there to assist you, not to replace you.

Visual Impairments

Divers who are blind or have other significant visual impairments will have special challenges with equipment inspections, including:

- Locating and identifying their gear. *Special adaptations*: Label gear conspicuously so your team can locate your gear. Place Braille labels on gear or other have other tactile configurations so you can locate your own equipment.
- Assessing equipment problems where tactile senses can pick up problems. *Special adaptations*: Practice tactilely inspecting your own gear to develop an understanding of what functional gear feels like. Feeling all equipment, mask lens and straps, BCD, regulator, purge buttons, inflator hoses etc. With practice you will have a better chance to detect equipment problems independently, seeking verification from your dive buddies.
- Inspecting equipment where sight is mandatory obviously requires dive buddy assistance: *Special adaptations*: If you can't read your gauges, you must ask your Adaptive Dive Buddy to give you a gauge reading to confirm if you have a full tank.

Physical Impairments

Similarly, if your physical impairment prevents you from turning on your tank valve, pressing low inflator buttons, or any other physical task related to the pre-dive safety check you must ask for help from your instructor or team.

If you have a mobility impairment that creates difficulty in examining whether a tank's O-ring is damaged or needs to be replaced, it is your responsibility to ask your dive buddies to position the tank so you can personally conduct an inspection. Moreover, if you are using a dive computer, confirm with your Adaptive Dive Buddy that the computer's self-diagnostics indicates a properly performing computer. If the low battery warning light is on, request assistance to have the battery replaced.

If you cannot independently inspect each piece of dive gear then you must solicit help to gather the gear and assess for abnormal conditions, defects and proper functioning.

Inspections of gear used for adaptive purposes must be performed well in advance of diving activities. Below is a list of commonly used gear and equipment used for adaptive diving. If you learn through your training that this equipment will be useful or necessary, then you should consider the following tips and guidelines for inspecting such equipment. For all equipment make sure you have reviewed the manufacturer's manuals for their instructions regarding inspection, safe operation and maintenance.

Adaptive Equipment Inspections

Descent Lines with anchor and buoy (Used for divers who need assistance with controlled ascents/descents)

Inspect the buoy for proper inflation and check whether the shackle attaching the line to the buoy is secured. Check the line for any fraying indicative of foreseeable breakage and confirm that the length of the line is adequate for the depth at the dive site. Check to make sure the anchor has the appropriate weight for the diving conditions and the type of bottom surface. If you are diving from a chartered boat, you can generally rely upon the captain and crew to perform the inspections for you, but you should verbally confirm that it has been done.

Full-Face Mask: (used for divers who cannot maintain a 2nd stage regulator in their mouth for underwater breathing or Visually-Impaired divers who wish to enhance their diving experience with underwater communications)

It is mandatory for you to review and understand the manufacturer's owner or operational manual for the specific mask you are using and perform any and all inspections accordingly. Generally, you want to inspect and confirm proper functioning of all buckles and releases, the 2nd stage demand valve, hose attachments, the face mask air vents, and whether the component parts for valsalva equalization are properly inserted and adjusted for your own personal use. Each manufacturer uses different devices and adjustments to block the nasal passageways for the valsalva.

During your pre-dive safety check of the Full-Face Mask, it is essential that you put on the Full-Face Mask to check for proper sealing and function of the unit. First check the Full-Face Mask with the air vent open, and then turn on your air supply. Thereafter close your breathing vent and check for proper functioning of the demand valve to make sure you are receiving adequate air. Also, during your pre-dive safety check you must confirm and re-confirm that you can effectively perform the valsalva, and if you need assistance confirm that your Adaptive Dive Team can effectively help you perform it. By taking this most important step during your inspection, you will enhance your chances of successfully equalizing and enjoying your dive.

For divers not capable of performing a bailout maneuver (i.e. removing the Full-Face Mask underwater and resorting to a conventional mask and regulator), the inspection must confirm that a redundant air supply valve is properly attached to the Full-Face Mask and pony tank, and all is functioning properly.

For divers using underwater communications, inspection and testing of all components of the audible system needs to be checked, including, batteries, battery compartments for signs of leakage, electronic contacts for oxidation, and system functioning—can you clearly transmit and hear communications.

Naturally, if you need assistance from another member of your team to conduct inspections you must confirm that your buddy has the knowledge and experience to provide assistance or you must be capable of carefully supervising and directing that assistance.

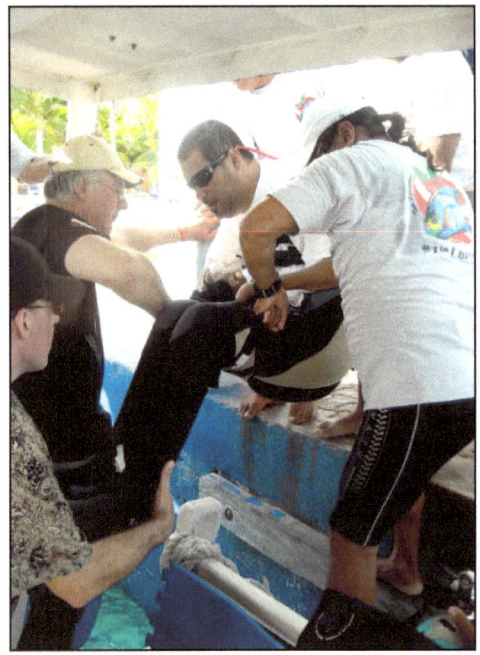

Transfer Harnesses: (used for transfers of physically impaired divers to and from the boat or dive site, and in and out of the water—particularly useful for large and heavy individuals)

A typical transfer harness resembles a soft gurney board and is made of some type of strong fabric, with multiple strap handles and buckles. Since it is foreseeable that four or more assistants may be involved in lifting you from a dock on and off boats and other challenging transfers, it is particularly important to inspect all component parts that must withstand the stress of carrying your weight. Look for any signs of abnormal wear and tear, including erosion of stitching material, handle attachments and all securing buckles and straps.

Ambulatory Devices: Walkers and Canes (used by physically impaired divers to assist with ambulation dockside and on the boat)

Although these devices are fairly simple in design and are easily inspected for abnormal conditions, it is worthy to note that the rubberized cushioned tips at the foot of canes and walkers can get worn out and slick. Since diving activities typically involve wet environments, it is important that you inspect the undersurface of rubberized tips to reduce the risk of slippage and falls.

Boat Wheelchairs and securing latches: (used by physically impaired divers to aid in transfers on and off boats and to serve as a secured dive seat)

Other than any regular inspection you would normally conduct, it is important to particularly inspect the parts of the wheelchair that assistants will grab during boat transfers. Four or more assistants may transfer you while you remain seated in the wheelchair on and off boats and other challenging transfers. Accordingly, you must inspect holding points for any defective

conditions that could result in breakage or other failures that could lead to a fall during the transfer. If your inspection raises any doubt that your wheelchair is not in condition for transfers, you should direct your dive buddies to perform an appropriate manual transfer.

Once your wheelchair has been transferred to the boat, you will need to be secure it using lashes; (typically) a weight belt strap onto a post, ladder or other fixed structure of the boat. This will provide you with a secured place to sit without the concern that the wheelchair may topple or move erratically due to wave conditions and other foreseeable boat movements. For this reason you must inspect the locking power of any buckle used for lashing.

Ankle Weights, Clip-ons and Weight Harness: (used by individuals whose physical features require weights to trim a diver for proper surface and underwater swimming orientation)

Generally, the inspection consists of determining if the clips and buckles are working so the weights will remain firmly attached and that the attaching points are free of defects, such as the D- rings and trim pockets of the BCD.

Prosthetic Fins: (used by divers with lower limb amputations)

As you can imagine, prosthetic fins are expensive and must be custom fitted to the amputee. A prosthetic swimming fin can cost up to $20,000 and therefore it is imperative that you review and follow the manufacturer's recommendations on proper inspections and use.

Swimming Gloves: (used by paraplegic and lower limb amputees divers for underwater swimming)

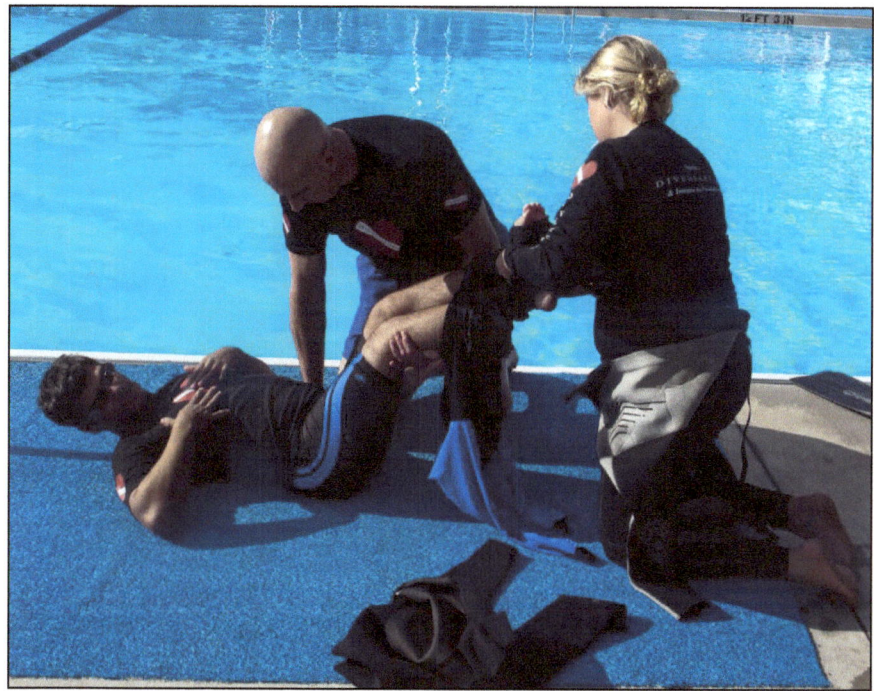

Full body skins and/or wet suits: (used by Adaptive Divers who have thermal regulation, sensory and physical impairments)

Inspecting these scuba-related garments is more involved than you might think. Just like the Full-Face mask, a proper inspection will include donning the wetsuit or diving skin. If you have thermal regulation deficits, or are diving in cold water, you will want to don the wetsuit to inspect whether you have a good seal at the neck, wrist and ankles and that the zippers are all functioning. Breaks in the seals at any of these potential areas of water entry will defeat the purpose of thermal protection. If you have sensory impairments in your limbs which may place you at risk for abrasions, stings, cuts etc, you should wear and inspect the garment to determine whether the wetsuit or skin fits and provides adequate coverage for skin protection.

If you have any physical impairments limiting normal range of motion of any joint (i.e. hips, knees, ankles, shoulders, elbows, and wrists) thereby adding difficulty to donning a wetsuit, then you need to inspect the wetsuit for its capacity to unzip and open up for easier entry of inflexible limbs. Even if you possess a custom wetsuit with long zipper lines it will be useless if the zipper is jammed by salt encrustations or debris. A careful inspection will avert having to cancel an otherwise beautiful day of diving.

Pressure Sore Mats and Cushions: (used by divers who have sensory impairments and are at risk for pressures sores)

These are relatively simple devices to inspect. However, there are some things you should specifically check out. Make sure the mat has not lost its cushioning properties. Some materials will compress overtime and lose their ability to provide pressure sore protection. Also, it is equally important to inspect the undersurface of the cushion or mat to determine if it has lost any anti-slip features. Using a mat that becomes overly slippery on a vessel's wet surface can be hazardous. You wouldn't want to use a slippery mat on the dive platform putting you at risk of sliding off the platform.

If you use swimming gloves, the most important aspect of the inspection is proper size and fit. Check out the finger webbing material for tears, rips or other defects.

General guideline for all Inspections

To the extent that you need assistance with any of these inspections, you should always discuss it during your pre-dive briefing—who, how, when and where inspections will be performed by your Adaptive Dive Team.

Donning and Removing Scuba Gear

Regardless of the nature or extent of your physical impairments, it is always your responsibility to know how to don and remove scuba equipment and wet or dry suit topside. Based on your guidance, your Adaptive Dive Buddies are there to render assistance to the extent you need them. They need your guidance for donning and removing gear since you know best how your physical impairments affect the way you generally dress yourself. If, for example, your left shoulder has limited motion, or causes pain beyond a certain range of motion, you need to let your dive buddies know and tell them the best strategy to help you don your scuba gear.

Mobility Impairments--Transfers and Positioning

If you have mobility impairments, it may be necessary to get assistance with transfers, donning scuba gear and to coordinate the movement of equipment to the dive platform. Usually several steps are involved.

You and your team will need to plan and coordinate this process. It usually requires more time and additional assistance to transfer the mobility-impaired diver in and out of his seat or wheelchair to adequately put on wetsuits. Consider how long it will take to travel to, and arrive at, the dive site so you know when to start the process of donning the wetsuit/dive skin and scuba gear. This is especially true if you have thermal regulation issues—you would not want to go through the effort of putting on a wetsuit on a hot day only to expose yourself to overheating.

Plastic bags placed over your hands and feet make donning dive skins and wetsuits easier. They make it easier to slide your limbs into the arm sleeves and pant legs. Readily accessible plastic grocery bags can serve this purpose.

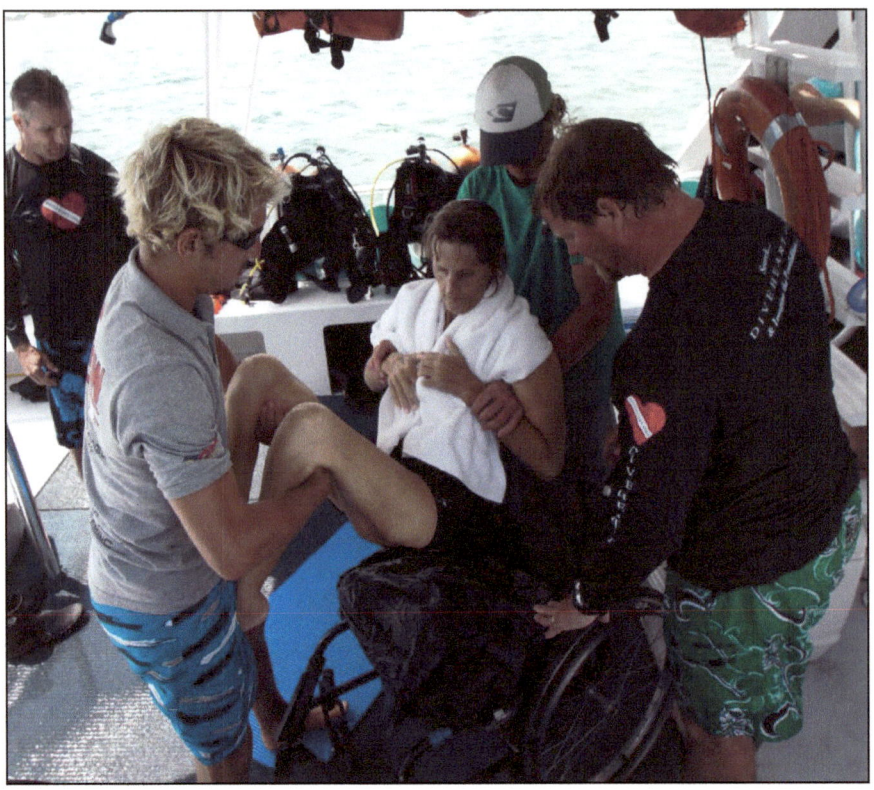

Your team may need to transfer you and your scuba gear to the dive platform for donning. Or you may need help putting on a wetsuit or dry suit while lying on a protective mat on the boat's deck. This should all be coordinated between you and your Adaptive Dive Team.

If you have a spinal cord injury or lesion, and are incontinent, you should be compliant with the bowel/urinary program, making sure collection bags are empty prior to diving. It is also important that you and your team exercise caution not to crimp any catheters that could cause urinary back up—a problem that could potentially trigger autonomic dysreflexia if your spinal cord lesion is at the T-6 level or above.

In order to perform a successful transfer to don scuba gear on the platform, you and your adaptive dive team must know how each of you will coordinate the following logistics:

- Who will assist in the transfer?
- How will the transfer be performed—which technique is best for you?

- Will you solicit boat crew or other support staff to assist?
- Will you need two or more people for the transfer?
- Does a dive buddy need to move a protective mat to the platform or other entry point?
- Who will transfer the scuba gear to the platform?
- Who will assist with donning all scuba gear, securing buckles, adjusting shoulder straps, etc?
- Who will be assisting with the predive safety check, if needed?

Other items to consider before transferring the Adaptive Diver:
- The boat's configuration and structures
- Narrow passageways, poles, low height clearances
- The dive environment as it relates to entries, exits and needed transfers to and from the dive entry point
- Clear passageways
- Before the transfer, you and your team need to determine the best route and check for any trip hazards or obstacles that could hamper the transfer
- Platform design; dive platforms vary in size, width and length and may have poles, ladders and other structures that may impede the transfer to certain portions of the platform
- Sea conditions may affect the balance of your adaptive dive team. If so, you may need additional spotters to provide support
- Your weight and height
- Any physical impairments that could impact the method of transfer
- Whether you have a limited range of shoulder motion or other painful conditions that would affect the lift and carry for the transfer
- Your preferred transfer method

If you require the use of a Full-Face Mask, you and your adaptive dive team must first be familiar with the specific unit before putting it on. If not, prior to diving activities you must procure the Manufacturers manual and become familiar with all operating functions including how to properly don and remove the Full-Face Mask. Generally you and your team should take the following steps:

1. First turn on tank valve and open the mask breathing vent before attempting mask placement
2. Secure the mask and obtain a proper seal with mask straps and buckle adjustments
3. Test the nasal blocking device to make sure you can effectively equalize ears and sinuses.
4. If your disability requires assistance for that test, determine who will be primarily responsible for assistance and how to perform it.
5. If the mask must be adjusted, make sure it is made and then check your ability to use the nasal device BEFORE the dive.
6. BEFORE entry, ensure (again) the air is on and then close the air vent to test the demand valve regulator to make sure you are receiving an adequate supply of air.

Sensory impairment

If you have sensory impairments, it is your responsibility to advise the dive team of any concerns related to numbness or hypersensitivity. You and your dive team should exercise care while using zippers to avoid catching skin that you might not otherwise feel. If you are placed on the boat deck to don a wet suit and the boat deck has an abrasive surface, you and your team must be careful not to drag your body against such surfaces to avoid abrasions.

If you are at risk for autonomic dysreflexia due to a spinal cord lesion or injury, your team must verify that none of your fingers or toes are bent (either hyper-flexed or hyper-extended) due to improper donning of the wetsuit. Similarly, you and the team should check for other sources of potentially painful stimuli that you may not readily feel but which could trigger hyper-reflexia. For instance, a full leg bag or crimped leg bag catheter could cause back flow precipitating an episode of autonomic dysreflexia.

Similarly, if you are at risk for pressure sores and will be placed on a hard boat deck or platform to don dive gear, you and your team should exercise caution by using appropriate cushioning material to reduce the development of skin breakdown or pressure sores.

Hearing Impairment

If you are hearing impaired and have no other disabilities, it is likely you will independently don your own gear. But if you have significant hearing and mobility impairments, you and your dive team will need to write out a predive briefing plan which will outline how the dive team will coordinate the dive and render assistance to you including everything required to help you take on and off your dive gear. Of course that may not be necessary if you are fortunate to have dive team members who can sign or you can effectively read lips. If not, all logistics that are outlined in the mobility impairment section should be written out describing how, who, when & where the team

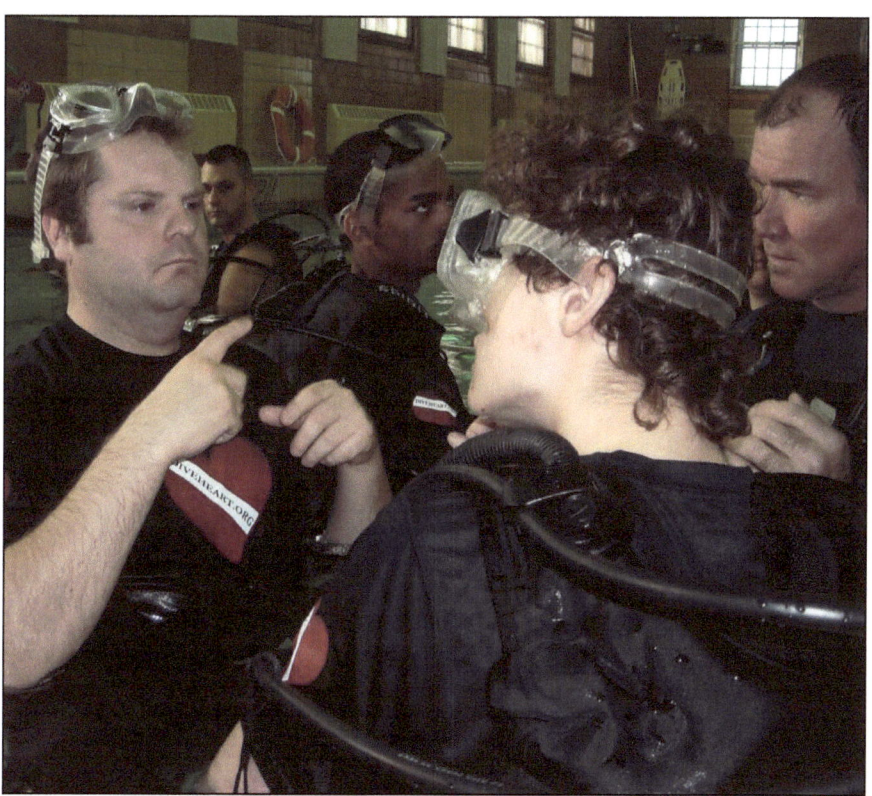

will coordinate to help you. To facilitate communications with you for donning and all other diving activities, Diveheart recommends that each member of the dive team use underwater writing slates.

Visual Impairment

If you are visually-impaired, there is a good chance that you will be able to don and remove your equipment independently with minimal to no assistance especially if you work hard practicing this skill. As with inspecting your scuba gear you need to use your tactile sense to become familiar with your gear and the location of each component part. Frequently practice the locations of the tank air valve, octopus rig, securing devices, mask buckles, BCD low pressure inflator hose and purge and inflate buttons, all buckles and fasteners of BCD, BCD purge valves, weight belt releases, integrated weight releases, etc. During the pre-dive briefing, the team should decide which Adaptive Dive Buddy will provide primary assistance with topside donning and removal.

Should you need to remove your equipment underwater, you and your team should develop some special hand signal to convey that there is a need to remove or re-don your equipment. During any underwater donning, you and one of your dive buddies should maintain constant contact so you are aware of their location and presence.

Becoming familiar with the scuba equipment for each of your team divers is also important. During the predive safety check, feel the scuba gear of your Adaptive Dive Buddies and develop the same understanding of the configuration and component parts of their gear. In the unlikely event that a team member needs your help to don or remove gear, you will be prepared to provide it.

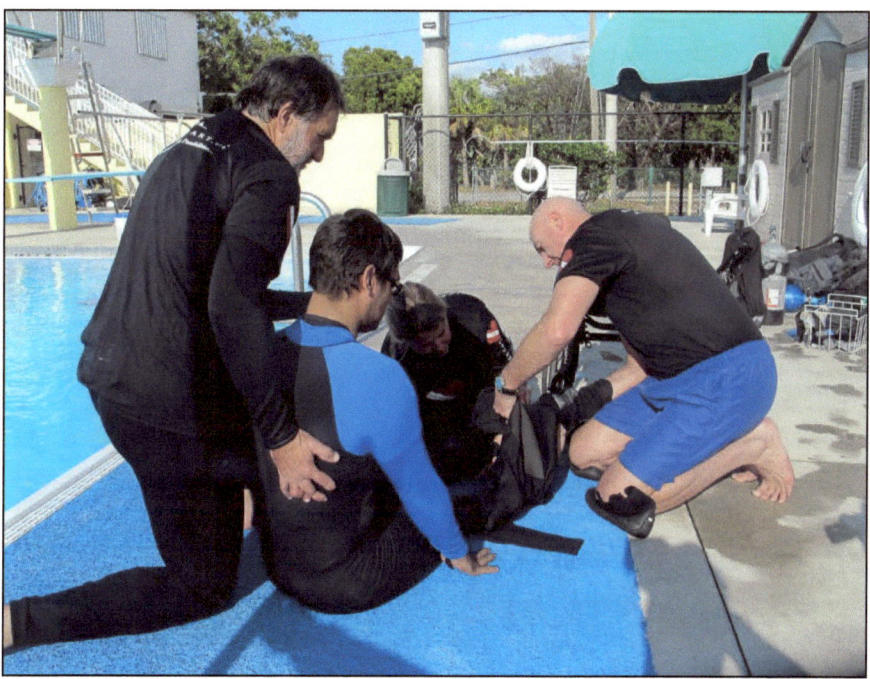

Thermal Impairment

In the event you have thermal regulation impairments, the most important consideration is when to start donning your wetsuit, dive skin or dry suits depending on whether you are prone to overheating or chilling. You will need to discuss with your team your tolerances for different temperatures and what type of activities or environmental conditions trigger thermal regulation problems.

If you are prone to hyperthermia, you will want to stay cool and postpone donning your wetsuit to minimize the risk of overheating on a warm sunny day. Knowing how much time it will take to get to the dive site is important so you can get the timing right. In the event you start to overheat after you have donned your wetsuit, you and your team can cool you down with wet rags, ice, fans, water spray or partially remove the wetsuit. Discuss these same considerations with your team if you are prone to hypothermia, but warming strategies will be used instead. Discuss and coordinate these considerations with the team during the predive briefing including who will provide primary assistance should you need help with thermoregulation.

Entries and exits

Depending upon the extent of your abilities you may require different forms of adaptation and varying degrees of assistance to enter and/or exit the water. Of course adaptations may not be necessary at all, if you are capable of performing a conventional entry, such as the giant stride. You will need to consider all the circumstances surrounding the entry point. For instance, do you need to travel over a sandy beach to enter the water or are do you need assistance with a transfer to the back of the boat in two to four foot seas. The level of assistance to enter and exit a pool may be vastly different from shore or boat diving. You should address the following:

- Can you wear scuba equipment while entering or exiting the water?
- What type of topside assistance will you need to enter the water depending upon the dive site? (i.e. entry from a shoreline, dive platform, poolside etc.)
- What type of in-water assistance will you need to exit the water?
- Will you don your gear at the water's edge or boat platform?
- Will you remove your gear in the water before exiting?
- Do you require assistance with transferring into or out of the water?
- Does your physical condition mandate donning and removing gear while in the water?

Regardless of the entry or exit scenario, it is very important to review your needs for assistance with your team and to work out who will be responsible for each task and how they will be sequenced. Additionally, you should review

these matters with any additional and qualified support staff that may be available on the shore or dive boat.

Mobility impairment /Entries

If you have a mobility impairments that require assistance to enter the water, the following techniques are recommended for a safe and effective entry. Which technique works best for you will depend on your abilities, preference and the circumstances surrounding the entry point.

Seated Front Roll: You can use this entry technique for poolside and dive platform scenarios. The seated front roll entry is performed by merely rolling forward into the water from a seated position. After donning your scuba gear, you need to be seated at the pool's edge or dive platform squarely facing the water. If you have weak arms or abdominal muscles which may affect your ability to remain in an upright position, let your team know so they can stabilize you. This is particularly important on a rocking dive boat.

A member of your dive team should be in the water prepared to assist you if you are not capable of floating vertically on the surface (that same in water diver can assist with putting on fins and ankle weights if needed):

- Reconfirm that your air is on and add adequate air to the BCD to maintain positive surface buoyancy
- Make sure one of your Adaptive Dive Buddies is positioned behind you and prepared to give you assistance with a forward push to help you and your tank clear the edge of the pool or dive platform
- Prepare for the entry by holding your face mask and second stage regulator so it doesn't become dislodged during the entry
- Have a dive team member do a 3-2-1 countdown so all members of the team can synchronize their assistance

- Just prior to the entry, make sure there is enough clearance for you to enter the water without hitting another diver including your in-water dive buddy.
- Countdown, bend and roll forward holding your mask and second stage regulator so it doesn't become dislodged during the entry.

For some divers it may initially feel strange since you may be upside down for a brief moment until you pop to the surface and get oriented or until your dive buddy gets you righted on the surface. With practice this will become second nature and comfortable to perform.

Modified Seated Front Roll: This technique is similar to the Front Roll, but instead of squarely facing the water you will be seated at a 45 degree angle. You will bend and roll onto your side than face. This will facilitate entry with minimal concern that the tank's bottom will not clear the platform or poolside. The same guidelines described above also apply to this maneuver.

The modified front roll may be more suitable in situations where there is not enough space behind you on the dive platform for your dive buddy to assist with a forward push and platform clearance. Also, many pools are designed in such a way that there is a narrow ledge along the perimeter requiring you and your tank to be seated at an angle due to limited space.

Manual Transfer Entry without Scuba Gear: Sometimes you may need to be manually transferred into the water from the boat or when approaching the dive site from a shoreline or beach.

For a beach dive, this technique involves a considerable amount of planning, multitasking and coordination among the dive team since you will be combining the maneuvers involved with a two step process of transferring you, and then your equipment into the water. Your team will need to assist you with donning your gear in water shallow enough for them to stand. After you are fully equipped and wearing your gear, each of your dive buddies or instructors will need to get their gear. Your dive buddies will need to take turns returning to the shore line to gear up while one of them remains with you to be available  for any needed assistance. Once everybody is together and fully equipped the team can complete their water entry and begin the dive.

If you do encounter this "entry" scenario, you and your team should perform the predive safety check before all the transfers to and from the shore line. You can imagine how frustrating it would be if after all the effort it took for the team to gear up to discover that somebody's tank was empty. Similarly, you and your team should discuss during the predive briefing the sequencing and coordination of the multitude of tasks required and how and who will provide the assistance.

Manual transfers, *without equipment,* from a boat may also be appropriate if you have significant upper mobility impairments involving both arms and/or a weak torso. With a diminished ability to steady yourself during pre-entry preparations or to secure your mask and regulator during entry, this option has some appeal. Like shoreline entries, this type of entry requires coordination and planning by the Adaptive Dive Team for all the same reasons.

Most importantly, after you have been transferred down into the water by the boat crew or other adaptive dive buddies, your two dive team members should already be in the water to receive you and provide necessary assistance with maintaining your surface buoyancy and donning your equipment.

One team member will be there to keep you afloat. Make sure that he has fully inflated his BCD to maintain the most positive buoyancy at the surface for both of you, while the other dive buddy fetches your gear from the dive boat. If you observe otherwise advise him to add air to his BCD. It is equally important to maintain a safe distance from the boat. If there is a current, the dive buddy maintaining your surface buoyancy should hold onto the boat's floating safety line to keep both of you from drifting too far from the vessel.

The other team member will then assist with putting on your gear. It is helpful if you face the dive buddy keeping you at the surface while the other dive buddy places the scuba gear on you. Loosening the shoulder straps or even releasing one strap will ease the donning of the BCD. It is also advisable to make the BCD only slightly buoyant since an overly buoyant BCD is difficult to don. During your training you will practice these maneuvers with your dive team and/or instructors until you are proficient and comfortable in executing this skill. Once you are fully geared up, you will have completed your entry and can start your dive.

Automated Transfer Entry without Equipment: (Hoyer lifts and other similar devices)

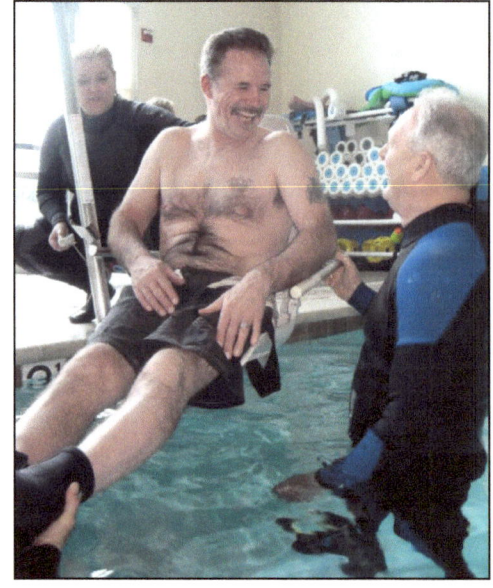

This technique uses special lifting equipment, like Hoyer lifts, to hoist you in and out of the water without your gear. Although commonly used in therapy pools, these lifts are generally not available on dive boats and other dive site entry points. However, it is possible to encounter Adaptive Dive Boat operations that do use this equipment where the boat does not have a dive platform or it is too high for safe entries. The boat crew familiar with the lifting device will provide instructions on how you will be lifted in and out of the water. Once you have been lowered into the water and received by your two awaiting team members, the procedures for completing the entry are the same as set forth in the above section relating to Manual Transfers.

Mobility Impairments/Exits

Just like entries, exits have to be carefully orchestrated between the team and support staff on the boat or shore. The extent of assistance with the exit will naturally depend on the nature and extent of your impairments. An example of a boat exit for a mobility-impaired diver who is unable to independently use the boat ladder would involve the following steps:

- Adaptive Dive Buddy team communicates it is time to exit the water.
- All team members add air for adequate surface buoyancy- a team member assisting with buoyancy control will inflate your BCD, if you need help

- If you require assistance to swim or maintain a vertical position with your head above water, one team member should stay behind you grabbing your tank or BCD to control your surface orientation and movements.
- The team works with you to remove your gear a safe distance, but not too far, from the dive platform at the stern of the boat. If there is a current, one of the dive buddies should secure the float line while removing equipment to prevent drifting too far from the boat.
- Removing your gear requires each team member to coordinate the sequencing of releasing the various straps and buckles—a topic that should've been discussed during the predive briefing. One dive team member should have the primary responsibility to remove your gear while the other maintains your surface buoyancy and provides swimming assistance.
- After your gear has been completely removed by one dive buddy and brought back to the boat, he will rejoin you and your other dive buddy to swim you to the dive platform for transfer out of the water.

Generally the best practice for out-of-water transfer to a dive platform will involve four qualified people—your two in-water team members who will lift you onto the platform from the water and two on the dive platform, also providing some lift and guiding you onto the platform.

- The Adaptive Dive team will swim you to the dive platform, with your back to the boat.
- The dive platform assistants will hold you under the arm pits.
- The in-water Adaptive Dive Buddy team synchronizes the start of the lift with a 3-2-1 countdown and drops below the surface while holding onto the dive platform.
    - They will push you up from below placing their hands on the backside of your upper thighs using the dive platform for leverage.

During the lift, the entire support team will guide you onto the dive platform. In the event you use a transfer harness, the same guidelines apply but your team will generally have grab handles to aid in the transfer.

Once seated on the platform with your legs still in the water, the next step is another synchronized transfer to move you further back to get you completely out of the water. Another 3-2-1 countdown will start this maneuver while the in-water team supports your lower legs and the platform assistants provide the additional lift to move you fully onto the platform.

Special Considerations for Full-Face Mask users during Exits

If you require a Full-Face Mask, it is important to attend to the mask properly before the exit. If the mask has a quick release permitting the second stage hose to detach from the Full-Face Mask, as with the Ocean Reef model, the mask should remain on you until you are transferred out. This will enable you to safely breathe on the surface. For obvious reasons, you and your team must be absolutely certain that your mask's breathing vent is opened fully before disconnecting the mask from the scuba unit. One of your team members should have primary responsibility to confirm that the breathing port is opened.

If the mask doesn't have a quick release, then the mask and the scuba unit will have to be removed at the same time. Once the scuba unit is removed, your team will transport you back to the boat for a transfer. During the swim back to the boat, your dive teams' BCDs should be maximally inflated so they can sustain easier surface flotation and keep your head above water. Even though they are trained to do so, if you perceive that they need greater flotation you should let them know. Remember this is a team effort and you should offer assistance to the extent needed and your capabilities.

Sensory impairment

If you have sensory impairments your capacity to feel pressure, sharp objects, pain, hot and cold surfaces, lacerations and other sensations maybe diminished to varying degrees. Accordingly, you should carefully survey the entry point for any potential conditions which may present a risk of injury. Similarly, if your condition places you at a risk of developing skin breakdown or decubiti ulcers from sitting on hard surfaces, then you will need to confirm that your dive team has first positioned an appropriately cushioned mat at the entry point to protect against these problems. Discuss the logistical details with your dive team during the predive briefing, including the following:

- who will move the protective mat to the point of water entry, and who will return it to the platform for the out of water exit
- who will then remove the mat and return it to you for continued use
- Are there shoreline or boat crew who can assist with the logistics

Hearing Impairment

If you have hearing impairments you will need to brief your adaptive dive team the extent of your capacity to hear verbal communications. Of course if your dive team can sign, you will have a tremendous advantage communicating underwater. If you are deaf or otherwise have significant hearing loss and your dive team cannot sign, you should prepare in writing your own predive briefing or request that your team leader prepare a written version for the entire team. The entry/exit methodology and logistics will need to be part of the written briefing along with all other topics that must be reviewed. Also, you should request the dive shop or boat captain provide copies of any written briefings regarding the safety features and other information concerning the dive site and dive boat which are customarily given verbally to their customers. Information regarding safe and effective water entries and exits are typically included in briefings. As an alternative to written briefings, there are a variety of apps for I-Phones and computer pads that transcribe verbal communications in real time.

Additionally, Diveheart recommends that you and your dive team all have underwater writing slates for additional surface communications including those needed for entries and exits.

Visual Impairment—Entry/Exit

If you are blind or have signification vision loss you will need your adaptive team to specifically describe the water entry and exit locations.

For shoreline or sandy beach approaches, have your team leader describe all aspects of the entry approach. During the pre-dive briefing review the following:
- the terrain that will be traversed
- any and all obstacles
- whether the surface is rocky, bumpy, or slippery, such that dive boots would be required
- the approximate distance to the entry point
- the depth of the water there
- whether any steps will be encountered
- all logistics involved in getting your equipment and the team's equipment

Remind your dive team that you depend on them for real-time verbal narration of what is occurring as you approach the entry and that you will be relying on them to lead you there. Your instructor and certified dive team have special training and experience assisting visually-impaired divers but you need to express any concern or request specific help any time you need it. As a general rule, you should maintain constant tactile contact with the dive buddy who will be providing primary assistance leading you to and from the entry and exit locations.

Proper weighting

Proper weighting is important for all divers to maintain buoyancy control and to stay properly oriented in the water, as well as swimming on the surface and underwater. If you have amputations, mobility impairments, paralysis, spasticity or there is any asymmetry to your body, it is likely you will tend to tip, roll, or pitch within the water column contrary to the way you may wish to move within it. This can be fixed by adding or removing weights strategically. By doing so you can offset the effects of the in-water imbalances your impairments may cause. Your instructor and dive team will work with you to determine the best placement for the weights for buoyancy control and proper swimming orientation.

A General Approach to Proper Weighting

Achieving proper weighting usually involves a three step process.

1. Don all of your gear and any wetsuits, dry suits or skins you may need for your dive. Determine the amount of weights you require by the methods described in your open water course (i.e. amount of weight necessary to float at eye level while holding a normal breath). As you float, take mental notes on how you tip, roll, pitch or are otherwise imbalanced.
2. Offset the tendency to tip, roll, etc. by trimming and adjusting the weight distribution. It's a process of adding, removing and shifting weights to achieve a balanced floating position.
3. Once a balanced floating position is achieved, descend underwater and determine if you can maintain a balanced swimming position where you are relatively horizontal in the water column. Sometimes you will detect additional imbalances that will require more trimming. For example, if you are a paraplegic and the ankle

weights added are too heavy you will have a difficult time maintaining a swimming position. After establishing balanced floatation and proper swimming orientations, recheck to make sure you are not over or under weighted.

> **Safety Tip**: **If you add weights for trimming it is critically important that sufficient weights can be quickly released for an emergency ascent or emergent need to acquire greater positive buoyancy at the surface.**

Achieving a proper trim can be a challenging and time consuming, but is essential for safe and enjoyable diving for you and your team. You and your instructor may need to be innovative and think out of the box to sort out proper weighting for you. Once you have determined how to make the necessary adjustments and the required amount of weights, as well as their strategic placements, make notes for future reference. You should specifically note the following:

- Whether proper and balanced weighting was achieved in fresh or saltwater
- The type and thickness of any wetsuit worn
- Descriptions of your tendency to roll, tip, etc., and the precise distribution of weights, their amounts and placements to offset the imbalances
- Any specialized weights used (e.g. ankle weights, clip-ons, etc.)

This information will be useful for your dive team if you will be requiring their assistance with proper weighting. Consider this information part of your unique adaptive diver profile—and discuss it during your predive briefing.

Mobility Impairments – Proper weighting

If you have significant mobility impairments—upper, lower or both—it is likely you will need assistance with proper weighting. Being properly weighted and trimmed out so you can maintain proper floating and swimming positions will greatly enhance safety and your enjoyment of the diving experience. It is also likely that if you have impairments you may need some assistance with controlled ascents/descents, and swimming on the surface or underwater. Your dive buddy will have to work much harder assisting you if you are persistently rolling, pitching, or not otherwise in a proper floating or swimming orientation. Not only will that tire your buddy, it will cause your dive buddy to deplete his air supply quicker, thereby, shortening your adaptive team's dive time. Bottom line—for you and your dive team's safety and enjoyment make sure your weighting is squared away.

Upper mobility impairments

If one of your arms is amputated or there is a significant difference in the size and weight of one arm compared to the other, you may have to add weight to the BCD's D ring on the side of the amputation or smaller arm.

If both arms are amputated you may have to add weights to upper and/or lower D rings on the BCD to get the trim right for comfortable swimming position. Sometimes you will have to add weight to the center of the BCD where there is no D ring. In this case you may have to add a clip on weight or ankle weight to a chest strap or waste band strap on the BCD.

If necessary, you can also add weights the wet suit arm sleeve if you fold the wetsuit sleeve back on itself and duct tape the suit together creating a loop in the sleeve. This will allow you to add an ankle weight to the sleeve.

Lower Mobility impairments

If you either or both legs are amputated, or the weight and size of either leg is different or you have paraplegia, you and your team may need to make adjustments and shift weights in accordance with the three step approach described above.

If you pitch forward too much, you may need to wear weights lower than normal to sustain a swimming orientation. Adding weights evenly distributed in the rearward BCD trim pockets may resolve the problem. Alternatively, you may try to attach an ankle weight to the lower portion of the BCD's frame or add weights to the tank strap or rear pocket holders.

If your feet tend to float up, consider using ankle weights. Try to use ½ pound or 1 pound ankle weights since anything heavier will drag your legs downward. If you can't obtain light ankle weights or if any ankle weight proves to be too heavy, try several types of fins. Different fins have different buoyancy characteristics and can make a sufficient difference in maintaining horizontal trim.

An additional method for attaching light trim weights to the leg is to fold the wetsuit's material over creating a pocket to add trim weights. Apply duct tape to fix the folded, weight filled pocket in place. Apply the duct tape to the wetsuit to create a loop as it is folded over on itself. Don't tape a weight itself to the wetsuit. You should always be able to jettison a weight if necessary or for transferring back to the boat.

Some ankle weights can be filled with shot and other materials and later emptied. This type of ankle weight is perfect for travel since there is no weight to them until you add the materials. It is ideal for fine tuning your trim since you can easily add or subtract the amount of weight needed. For example you may only need a half a pound/quarter kilogram on one leg and a pound and a half/three quarter kilogram on the other leg.

If both legs have no functional capacity, you and your dive team may consider joining your legs together making your underwater profile more symmetrical, thereby making proper weighting easier. This will help you better protect your legs and create better hydrodynamics for underwater and surface swimming. If your legs are dangling, there is a greater risk they may inadvertently come into contact with the underwater environment. This poses a risk of injury to you if your legs are not fully protected by a skin or wetsuit, and further poses an ecological risk to sensitive marine organisms such as corals.

Total Mobility Impairment

If you have quadriplegia, or have no arms or legs, your instructor and dive team will provide you the necessary assistance to achieve proper weighting. The same general approach and weighting strategies apply to you as described in the previous sections. There are some special considerations for your situation.

If your arms and legs have no functional capacity, you and your dive team may consider joining your limbs together making your underwater profile more symmetrical and proper weighting easier. Also, by doing this, you can better protect your limbs and create better hydrodynamics for underwater and surface swimming. If your arms or legs are dangling there is a greater risk they may inadvertently come into contact with the underwater environment. This poses a risk of injury to you if your limbs are not fully protected by a skin or wetsuit, and further, poses an ecological risk to sensitive marine organisms such as corals.

You can join your limbs with blank weight belts for the legs and large elastic wrist bands for your arms. By joining your limbs together, you will also create a more hydrodynamic profile reducing the water resistance your dive buddy is confronting when providing underwater swimming assistance to you. Also, as an incidental benefit to joining your legs with a blank weight belt, your dive buddy will have a singular handle to hold both legs in a horizontal swimming orientation.

Another piece of adaptive equipment is a neoprene band with Velcro which could also be used to hold your legs together. The neoprene band is softer than a blank weight belt and if the Velcro patch is long enough, it can be adjustable for a variety of sizes needed. It is an effective and gentle way to keep legs together.

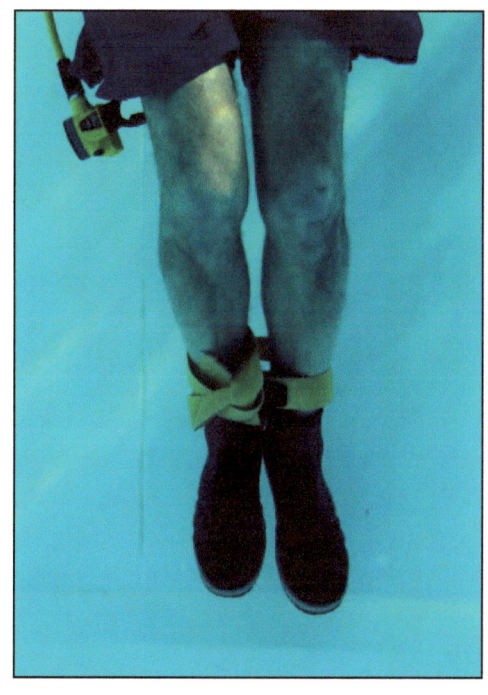

If you have no arms or legs, you are more symmetrical than someone who has fewer amputations. Because you don't have to counterweight to accommodate for an arm or leg, you will be able to focus on weighting the torso. You will probably need a variety of weights to accomplish this including ankle and clip-on weights. Since a weight belt may slip off your waist, the weights can be alternatively attached to your tank. Another option is the vest type weight harness which is easy to adjust, and trim for proper weighting.

Sensory impairment

For divers who have sensory loss, as well as divers who may be at risk for autonomic dysreflexia, it is important to exercise caution to not apply too much pressure by placing weights or tightening straps against the body which can provoke painful stimuli. If ankle weights are too tight, they may cause skin breakdown or decubitus ulcers or may even trigger autonomic dysreflexia. You and your team should discuss these important precautionary guidelines at all predive briefings so your team can provide proper and safe assistance for all weighting scenarios.

Visual Impairment

If you have visual impairments that impact your ability to get weighted appropriately in accordance with the guidelines outlined here, your instructor and dive team will assist you so you can sucessful accomplish this skill. Once you and your team have acheievd proper weighting, use your tactile senses to feel all the weights, clip-ons, ankle weights, their attachment, releases mechanisms, placements, and any quick release features for each. Practice as often as possible so you can perform proper weighting with minimal assitance.

Thermal Impairments

If you have thermal impairments it is not likely your ability to get weighted appropriately will be affected. However, if you are prone to hypothermia, it's likely you will use a wetsuit more often than most and may need a thicker wetsuit. Thicker wetsuits will certainly affect your buoyancy, especially ones that are customized to account for amputations and other physical changes in body symmetry.

Note: Dive Planning for Proper Weighting: As mentioned earlier, it may take more time than you may realize to achieve proper and balanced weighting for Adaptive Diving. It will be quite frustrating for you and your team if after all the effort to get to the dive site you discover that you are over or under weighted or relentlssly fighting to keep from rolling to the right because of a weighting issue. You and your team must discuss and deal with weighting in a timely fashion.

A meaningful pre-dive briefing with your dive team should include a review and discussion of the following items:

- How much weight you require
- The need for trimming due to impairments
- The need for special weights for trimming (e.g. ankle weights, clip-ons etc.)
- How to distribute and attach weights to effect trimming
- Who will primarily assist you with proper weighting
- Where and when will proper weighting occur before the dive
- Who will procure the weights needed

- Whether special precautions need to be observed due to sensory impairments

Weight/ballast system- underwater removal and replacement

Mobility impairments

If you have upper mobility impairments, you and your team will need to assess your capacity to perform this skill independently. If you do not have any functional use of either arm, or weakness, lack of dexterity, spasticity or paralysis and that prevents you from manipulating your integrated BCD weights for removal or replacement, or prevents you from putting on and off your weight belt, you will require assistance from your team. Ensure that your dive team  knows how to work the quick release mechanisms of your particular BCD. Since one of the reasons for knowing how to remove a BCD underwater is in response to an emergency situation, you don't want your dive team to be fumbling around trying to locate and operate the quick release. Also, the team needs to coordinate the removal and/or replacement of the weights. One dive buddy should provide primary assistance with removal and replacement of the weights while the other dive buddy assists with buoyancy control and underwater swimming. The second Adaptive Dive Buddy should be prepared to make timely adjustments to his buoyancy and yours to avoid an uncontrolled ascent.

If you have lower mobility impairments only, you should be capable of removing and replacing your own weights. But if you require some assistance with buoyancy control or underwater swimming, your dive team will need to coordinate in a similar fashion. During the pre-dive briefing, you should review and confirm that the entire team is familiar with the release mechanisms as discussed above and who will be providing primary assistance for these skills.

Visual Impairments

Should you have visual impairments, you should be able to independently remove and replace weights underwater. To do so, you will need to first become familiar tactilely with the release mechanisms of your BCD integrated weights and/or weight belt. With sufficient practice you should have no problem performing this skill.

If there is a need to remove your weights underwater, you should work out a special tactile hand signal with your dive team to signal that weights need to be removed. You might need to do this if you need to add or remove weights if you are over-weighted or under-weighted. Your dive team must be ready to provide assistance with your buoyancy control. As a visual impaired diver, it is sometimes difficult to perceive your rate of ascent, and your dive buddy needs to make appropriate adjustments to your buoyancy. Dive with a dive computer that provides an audible alarm for unsafe ascent rates. Should you accidentally drop your weights, for example, the audible alarm will trigger your need to dump air.

Hearing, Sensory and Thermal Impairments

These impairments should not cause any difficulty in performing this skill, and therefore no adaptations or special assistance should be required.

Mouthpiece clearing - snorkel and regulator

To scuba dive safely, it is obvious that you must be fully capable of breathing underwater. After all, your scuba gear is literally life support equipment that allows you to explore an underwater environment that is not naturally suitable for humans. This means you must have full physical capacity to maintain a regulator in your mouth and be capable of purging any water that may enter your 2nd stage regulator by forced exhalation or use of the purge button.

Similarly, safe use of a snorkel requires the ability to secure the mouth piece and to clear any excess water. After your instructor demonstrates how to clear the snorkel and regulator, you will work together to determine your ability to perform these skills. If you cannot maintain the regulator mouthpiece in your mouth for breathing, you will be required to use a Full-Face Mask. A Full-Face Mask also has features allowing for swimming on the surface without a snorkel. The Full-Face Mask is a wonderful piece of adaptive gear that will enable you to go diving. It virtually eliminates the elevated risk of drowning that would otherwise be there for a diver who would have difficulty clearing or maintaining a regulator.

If you do need a Full-Face Mask, you will learn more about the skills related to its use, including how to clear it, and how your team will provide assistance in a later section.

The next section will review adaptive techniques, special gear, and dive team assistance for those adaptive divers who can effectively use their mouthpieces.

Mobility impairment

If you have upper mobility impairments that affect your ability to perform regulator or snorkel clearing, try the following guidelines, techniques, and tips. If you have muscle weakness, partial paralysis, spasticity or similar conditions, practice repeatedly until you can proficiently and timely place the regulator and snorkel in your mouth and successfully purge the water.

If not successful, your Adaptive Dive Team can provide assistance to guide and place the regulator into your mouth. If you are capable of pushing the purge button or can clear with forced exhalation, you should do so; otherwise your dive buddy can do it for you. If you or your buddy clears the regulator using the purge button, use your tongue as a splash guard. If this procedure effectively works, you and your dive team will need to decide during the pre-dive briefing who will provide primary assistance. It should be the same team member who provides primary assistance with regulator recovery since clearing the regulator is part of that skill.

If you have any concerns whether you can successfully and proficiently perform this skill with or without assistance, or you are unwilling to accept the risk of drowning if you are not capable of consistently performing this skill, consider using a Full-Face Mask.

Similarly, if you cannot use both arms due to complete paralysis or double amputation, you are faced with an elevated risk for drowning while using conventional regulators. This is true even if you can maintain your regulator in your mouth.

Although misplacement of your regulator's mouth piece represents an unlikely event, and your Adaptive Dive Team is trained and experienced at addressing these scenarios, the elevated risk of serious injury and death still exists. Accordingly, Diveheart strongly recommends Full-Face Masks for such divers. A Full-Face Mask significantly reduces that risk. If you are willing to accept the elevated risk, and you have determined that your Adaptive Dive Team can properly assist you while using a conventional regulator, including assisting you with out-of-air emergencies, then you can decide which equipment would be acceptable to you.

Diveheart's Mandatory Rules for Full-Face Mask Usage and Related Equipment

For any diver who is not capable of keeping a regulator's mouth piece in place in order to safely breathe underwater, Diveheart requires the Adaptive Diver to use a Full-Face Mask during all dive training activities. Additionally, if any diver cannot perform a Full-Face Mask bailout procedure due to any impairment, the Adaptive Diver will also be required to attach a redundant air supply valve to the Full-Face Mask.

Adaptive Divers requiring this equipment will need to carefully read the sections in this manual that cover Full-Face Mask use, redundant air supply valve, bailout procedures and related dive team protocols. During your training you and your dive team will learn how to assemble, operate and use Full-Face Mask equipment and how the team will assist you. Upon completion of the Adaptive Scuba Course your certification will be conditioned on you using that equipment.

Visual Impairments

If you have any type of visual impairment, complete blindness, or otherwise, you should have the capacity to perform mouthpiece clearing with either a regulator or snorkel. As with all other diving activities, you need to get well acquainted tactilely with your regulator and its purge buttons and practice until you can do the skill in a repeatable and consistent way. If you feel that your dive team can render assistance in some way, review and discuss how it should be performed and who will give primary assistance during the pre-dive briefing.

Lower Mobility, Sensory and Thermal Impairments

Impairments, including complete lower extremity paralysis and double leg amputations, should not affect your capacity to perform mouthpiece clearing so generally there is no need for adaptations.

Snorkel Clearing:

For all Adaptive Divers who may require assistance with regulator mouth piece clearing, you probably will need similar assistance with your snorkel while at the surface. Although there are no purge buttons that your team can assist you with, you can always use a snorkel that features an automatic purge valve eliminating water by simply exhaling.

Regulator/snorkel exchanges and Surface Swimming

General Protocols for All Impairments

If you are able to perform the mouthpiece clearing skills with or without assistance, you should be capable of performing regulator-snorkel exchanges at the surface. You will need to practice the placement of the snorkel's mouth piece in your mouth to acquire a level of confidence that you can do it consistently and proficiently with the aid of your dive buddies. In wavy sea conditions you will want to perform this skill in a quick and timely way. It is always a good practice to maintain maximum buoyancy while at the surface while using your snorkel to help keep the snorkel elevated above the waves. If you observe that any of your Adaptive Dive Buddies have not adequately inflated their BCD take the initiative to remind them. Remember the entire experience is a team effort.

Surface-snorkel swimming with full diving system

Upon returning to the surface after a dive, you may need to switch to your snorkel and swim on the surface to get closer to the boat. To the extent you cannot do this independently, you and your team will practice the special procedures for coordinating the surface swim with each member of the dive team depending upon the extent of your needs.

If you require assistance with buoyancy control or swimming at the surface, make sure your team understands your special needs and who will provide primary assistance. As a general protocol, divers requiring assistance with underwater swimming will most likely require similar assistance with surface swimming. One of your dive buddies should be primarily assigned the task to assist you with maintaining a vertical orientation on the surface while treading, if your impairment makes that challenging. The same dive buddy should assist with surface swimming using the tired diver tow (push tow or pull tow). The second dive buddy can provide supplemental assistance if needed.

Selection of the Primary Swimming Assistant

For all swimming activities, surface or underwater, you and the dive team should decide who is best suited and physically fit to serve as the primary dive buddy for swimming assistance. That dive buddy should be reasonably comfortable with all types of diving conditions and capable of handling the associated physical stress of foreseeable challenging environmental conditions while providing swimming assistance. The selected dive buddy should be fit, confident and capable to handle waves, cold and warm water temperatures, currents, winds, rain, thermoclines, surf, underwater surge, and distance swimming. This buddy should be capable of controlling his buoyancy control while providing assistance to your buoyancy to the extent you need it.

This topic should be discussed during the predive briefing together with the mouth piece clearing procedures. Since these diving maneuvers involve similar skills, the same dive buddy should be providing primary assistance for both.

Underwater "Gravity Free" Swimming

Depending on your physical impairments and abilities, you may not need assistance with underwater swimming. Some Adaptive Divers are able to move through the water using webbed gloves, for example. They may only need assistance with swimming in situations where there are currents or when they become tired. If you have significant mobility deficits, you will learn about how your dive team will coordinate with you to provide assistance with underwater and surface swimming.

The general protocol for underwater swimming for more severely impaired divers is designed so one member of the team is primarily responsible for moving the diver thru the water column and assisting with buoyancy control while the other manages effective communications with you and the other adaptive dive buddy. You will also learn the importance of good buoyancy control and horizontal positioning in the water to reduce the amount of work required to move through the water.

Perhaps one of your goals is to swim underwater independently. It is exhilarating to be in a weightless environment that only the underwater world can provide. It is as exciting as it is therapeutic. Regardless of your abilities you will enjoy the experience of flying free and moving about better than you have ever experienced before. Even if you need underwater swimming assistance, there will always be an opportunity for you to enjoy the thrill and physical freedom of flying in a gravity-free world. Your Diveheart Adaptive Scuba Instructor will help you reach that goal to the greatest extent possible.

Your Adaptive Dive Team is present to render assistance to the extent you need them. If you need assistance adjusting buoyancy while swimming or moving horizontally or vertically through the water, you and your team can work out a plan on how each member will provide assistance. If you are using a Full-Face Mask and need assistance with equalization while swimming, special signals can be used so your team can address your needs by coordinating with each other. Special protocols and considerations relative to underwater swimming as they relate to different impairments are more fully described in the next section.

Swimming Positions of the Adaptive Dive Team

As discussed earlier, the Adaptive Dive Team protocol is nothing more than an enhanced version of the buddy system. The core principal is to stay close to your dive buddy so you can help each other and to share the fun and joy of diving together.

With Adaptive Scuba, the dive buddies will provide greater help and each will have their own set of ***primary assistance roles*** for different scuba skills. Providing assistance can be easier and more effectively done from certain positions. As an Adaptive Diver, who may need varying degrees of assistance, it is good to know where your dive buddies will be positioned around you. Although the overriding rule is to do whatever is best for safety, effectiveness and enjoyment, Diveheart recommends the following general strategies and protocols for the swimming positions of your adaptive dive team:

Adaptive Diver's Swimming Positions/Orientation

To the extent you require assistance with underwater swimming and other scuba skills during your dive, your adaptive team will also provide assistance making sure that you are properly oriented in the water. For instance, if due to your impairments you need to be righted and placed vertically at the surface following your water entry, your team will be there for these maneuvers. Or, if you are paraplegic and your feet are about to drag onto the ocean bottom, your dive buddy can pick up your legs so you are in a more horizontal orientation.

Generally, during descents, ascents and safety and/or rest stops your team will place you in a comfortable vertical position. While swimming, your team will position you in a primarily horizontal swimming position, not only for comfort but to reduce water resistance so your dive buddies do not have to work too hard. Their positioning around you is generally related to the type of assistance they will be providing.

Adaptive Dive Buddy--Rearward Position

If your Adaptive Dive Buddy is providing assistance with underwater swimming, surface swimming, buoyancy control, controlled descents/ascents, regulator recovery, safety/deco stops, or monitoring your gauges, he will generally be positioned behind you and to your right-side. At times, especially during ascents/descents, or at the surface, he may be more directly behind you either straddling your tank with his knees or holding the tank's top and bottom to exercise better control. During relatively horizontal underwater swimming, he may also stay directly behind you to better propel you thru the water.

Adaptive Dive Buddy--Forward Position

If your Adaptive Dive Buddy is providing assistance with equalization, out-of-air emergencies, mouthpiece clearing, standard mask or Full-Face Mask clearing, mask removal, replacement or clearing, regulator/snorkel exchanges at surface, and signaling between you and him, he will generally be in a forward position.

Upper Mobility Impairments

If you have upper mobility impairments and at least one leg is functional, you have the capability to swim underwater independently. There are plenty of boats that navigate the seas with one prop. This does not mean you will not be challenged.

During pool sessions it will take time to learn how your body can move through the water once you have established neutral buoyancy. Even without full use of your arms, you can learn how to move to the right or left, ascend or descend, by making adjustments with your torso and finning techniques that work. Watching seals darting thru the water will give you an idea how this can be done. Properly using breath control to assist with up and down movements can be quite effective. It's all a matter of experimenting and practice. Spend time during pool sessions trying different movements which may help you move thru the water.

If you have some function in either arm, try webbed swimming gloves or hand fins to enhance the power of your swimming strokes.

If you have an arm amputation and have sufficient stumps for prosthetic application, there are prostheses specially designed for swimming that can significantly improve your underwater capabilities.

If you have very little function in your arms, and need assistance with equalization and buoyancy control during underwater swimming, you and your Adaptive Dive Team should work out a plan to coordinate when and how they will provide assistance.

Lower Mobility Impairments

If you have paraplegia, lower limb amputations, or other lower mobility impairments, you still have the ability to effectively swim on the surface and underwater. If your legs are not capable of generating enough kick to move you through the water, your swimming arms can certainly do the job.

To enhance the thrust of your swimming strokes there is a variety of adaptive gear, including different types of web gloves, hand and forearm fins, as well as prosthetic swimming arms. These are wonderful tools that will enable you to independently swim. If you choose to use adaptive gear or prosthetics, your Adaptive Dive Team should stay close but not so close that they interfere with your arm strokes. Similarly, you will need to exercise caution that your sweeping arm strokes do not accidentally strike your dive buddies dislodging their regulators or mask, or sensitive marine life.

Additionally, you and your team may need to formulate special signaling if using these devices prevents you from signaling or otherwise communicating with your dive buddies. Clearly, it would be difficult to use conventional hand signals or write on a dive slate while wearing web gloves. For instance, if you need assistance with buoyancy control, you will need to create a special signal conveying your need for assistance and each dive team member must agree to its use.

Complete Mobility Impairment

If you have quadriplegia, or have no arms or legs, most people will probably think you are absolutely incapable of scuba diving. The notion is understandable--but wrong. So long as you are willing to accept the significantly-elevated risk of drowning and the other known risks of scuba, your Adaptive Dive Team can provide the necessary assistance for you to experience the freedom of weightlessness and to explore the wonders of the underwater world.

Due to the severity of your mobility impairments, and the elevated risk of drowning, injury or death, it is strongly recommended that you use a Full-Face Mask for all scuba diving activities. Your adaptive dive team will be providing all the assistance you will need to navigate and move thru the aquatic environment. Just sit back and enjoy the gravity free experience.

Your primary responsibility during your dive is to effectively communicate or signal your Adaptive Dive Team regarding any assistance you may require. This can be easily accomplished by using Full-Face Mask with underwater radio communications. Even with these devices you will need to develop a special system of signaling that all members of your dive team understand so you can be prepared for the possibility of communication device failure.

Special signaling can be created by using different combinations and sequences of eye blinks and head movements. Generally, you want to create signals that are initiated by your Adaptive Dive Buddy which represents a question relative to whether or not you need assistance with a particular scuba skill that will require a simple "Yes" or "No" signal from you. There is no standardized set of signals for this. What is important is that you and your dive team agree and understand all the signals before the dive—an absolutely mandatory topic to be reviewed at the pre-dive briefing.

The following is a recommended set of special signals you may wish to use, or tweak them to best serve you and your team:

Are you OK? Adaptive Diver Buddy points to you & presents OK signal. You respond with a Yes nod or No nod.

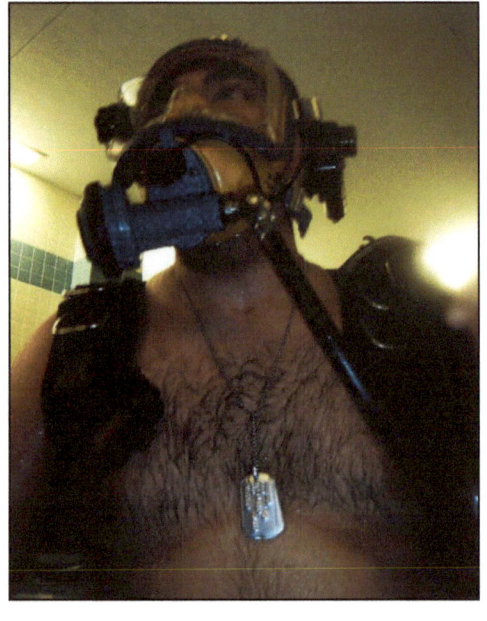

If you are out of air, you will give a rapid and continuous No nod or eye blinks until air supply is restored. (Note: In the event of an out-of-air emergency, your Adaptive Dive Buddy will switch the redundant air supply valve to your alternative air supply or will initiate the bailout procedures— see Full-Face Mask -Out of Air Procedure section for more information).

If "no" the Adaptive Dive Buddy will then go thru a sequence of signals to find out what is wrong. The Adaptive Dive Buddy will first present the standard "what's wrong signal" (e.g. hand fingers fanned out and flapping hand with rotational gyrations) and then point to different parts on himself to signify the following potential problems:

- Points to his ear—to determine if there is an ear equalization problem.
- Points to head and grabs top of head—to determine if you are experiencing symptoms consistent with autonomic dysreflexia or severe headaches.

- Points to stomach and gives standard ascent signal—to determine if diver wants to return to surface due to any reason relating to not feeling well enough to continue the dive (e.g. fatigued, too cold, feeling sick, etc.)
- Points to you and then presents standard "I'm Cold" signal—to determine if you are cold
- Points to you and then "tired sign"—to determine if your are physically tired or fatigued
- Points to you and gives standard ascent signal—to determine if you desire to stop diving and return to the surface for any reason other than not feeling well.
- Points to your mask's face plate – to determine if there is a need to clear your Full-Face
- Mask Points to your mask's strap—to determine if Full-Face Mask straps require adjustment

In response, you must clearly signal with a "Yes" or "No" nods of the head, or a one eye blink for "Yes" or two eye blinks for "No". Based upon your response, your dive buddy will provide the appropriate assistance. If your response indicates you are having a problem equalizing, your Adaptive Dive Team will help you clear your ears.

For situations where your Adaptive Diver Buddy does not initiate the signaling, but you need to get your dive team's attention that there is something wrong, give three nods of the head and pause for five seconds and repeat this sequence until your Adaptive Diver Buddy responds except if you are having an out-of-air emergency, in which case you will continuously nod "No" until air supply is restored. Other than out-of-air emergencies, the Adaptive Diver Buddy will then start the sequence of signaling as described above.

You and your dive team may decide to adopt the recommended signals, modify them or create your own set, but you must develop them, agree upon them and be certain that all team members understand them. It is important that whatever signaling system you use, that it must cover, at a minimum, standard signal communications and the type of communications referenced above. You and your dive team must not only discuss this topic during the predive briefing but must practice each signal and response to confirm that everybody is presenting their signals clearly. Sometimes an emphatically presented signal will be necessary. For example—BIG nods of the head.

Signaling Recommendations for Other Physical Impairments

For divers who do not have complete mobility impairments, special signals are just as important. You and your team will need to develop your own system of communicating during your dive. Many of the signaling recommendations described in the preceding section can certainly be used. ==MOST IMPORTANTLY MAKE SURE ALL SIGNALS ARE DISCUSSED AND DEMONSTRATED DURING THE PREDIVE BRIEFING.==

Visual Impairment- Underwater swimming

Most people believe, understandably, that what makes scuba diving so fantastic is the visual beauty and sights of the underwater world. Blind divers with experience, however, will tell you that there is a lot of enjoyment and benefit in the scuba experience. Gravity-free swimming alone is worth the effort, not to mention the thrill of listening to new sounds generated by marine life and other underwater audible noises—especially with the heightened sensitivity of a blind diver's hearing. Other Visually-impaired divers report the remarkable sense of dimensionality, feeling the presence of the reef or the depths below them. Perhaps more important than all of that is the consistent reporting by blind divers of how empowering the experience is to their self esteem and confidence. Many of them will exclaim "If I can Scuba Dive, then I can do anything. Don't tell me anymore that I can't do this or that."

If you are blind or visually-impaired you should remain in tactile contact with one of the two members of your Adaptive Dive Team when swimming underwater. The dive buddy providing primary assistance for communication will hold onto your right hand during the entire dive if you are totally blind or have very little vision. If you are visually-impaired to a lesser degree, you may

be capable of swim independently using the vision you have to stay close to your Adaptive Dive Team.

As a visually-impaired diver you may want to "see" things by touching them. It is important to know what is safe to touch and what is not. Dee Scarr's book, *Touch the Sea*, is a good reference to prepare you for the dive.

A Full-Face Mask with communications can also enhance your diving experience. This can give you a greater sense of independence since your Adaptive Dive Buddy can give you clock references to navigate through the water and your buddy can give real time narration describing the dive.

Your dive team must have excellent buoyancy control and heightened situational awareness to guide your underwater swimming so you do not accidently run into marine life and sunken structures that could cause injury to yourself or damage to the marine environment.

For this reason it is important to conduct a thorough pre-dive briefing and have a plan that addresses tactile communication and all other assistance you will need as a visually-impaired diver.

If you have a visual impairment to the extent that that you cannot see signals initiated by your dive team, then you will learn how to communicate tactilely with special signals outlined below. Regarding other visual

impairments such as loss of central or peripheral vision, blurred vision, blind spots, double vision and varying visual acuity disorders, you may still have some useful vision to see signals depending on how they are presented and proximity of presentation. You will need to educate your team on how to best present signals depending upon your specific ocular condition. For example, if you have a visual field loss where you can only see objects that appear in the upper right quadrant of your visual field, then you will show your dive buddies where they need to present the signal for you to see it. Consulting with your team in this way will enable you to effectively communicate underwater.

Hand signals for Visually-Impaired Divers

The following signals are used to communicate directly underwater. Your Adaptive Dive Buddy will hold your right wrist to communicate that a signal is coming:

- OK: Your buddy will squeeze your right hand once
- Problem: Multiple squeezes to your right hand
- Mistake: Erase a sign with a circular motion applied to your right palm face up
- Descend: Pressure applied to back of your hand with one finger.
- Ascend: Pressure applied to palm of your hand with one finger.
- Get Neutral: Circular motion applied to back of hand, followed by "ascend" if too negative, by "descend" if too positive.
- Regulator Recovery: A squeeze on your right shoulder, with a gentle tap on your regulator

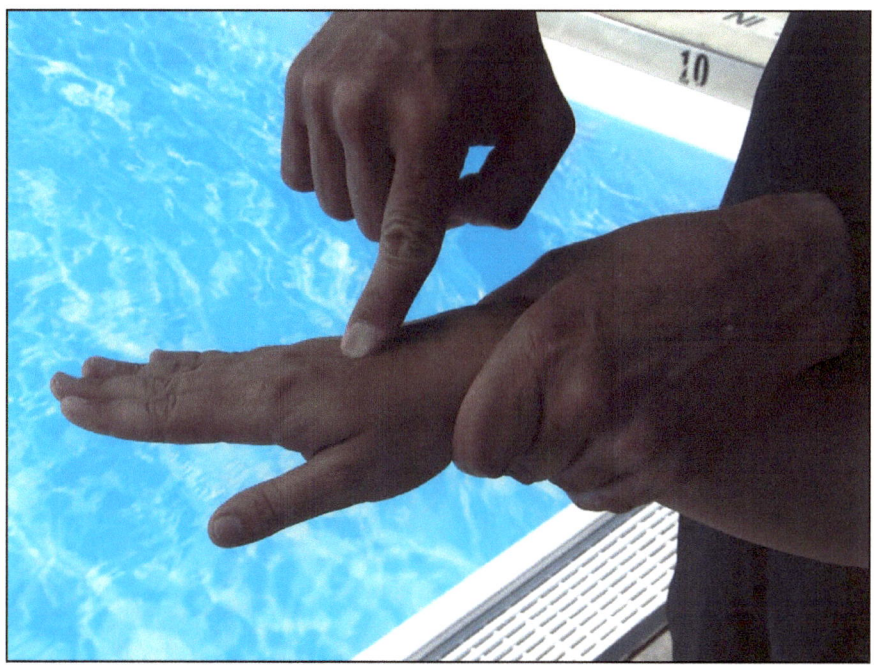

- Out of Air: A tap on your chest, if you are out of air, or use your hand to tap on your buddy's chest to reverse out-of-air signal.
- Gauges: Air, Depth and Time: Your buddy will hold your right wrist and trace a circle (indicating gauge reading) on palm of your hand with finger.
- Air Pressure: Hold right wrist, Trace circle on right palm, followed by one squeeze (your air), one squeeze on the thumb = 1,000 psi AND one squeeze on the index finger = 100psi.
- Depth: Hold right wrist, trace circle on right palm, followed by pressure to back and palm of hand (pinching motion). Your buddy will squeeze your thumb for every 10 feet/3m./ and your index finger for each additional foot.
- Time: Hold right wrist, trace circle right palm, followed by squeeze to wrist. Your buddy will count time by squeezing thumb for every ten minutes and index finger for single minutes.
- Add air: squeeze right index finger
- Dump air: Pull right index finger
- Remove and Replace BCD underwater …tap BCD waistband or buckle

- Controlled Emergency Swimming Ascent: Tap on chest of visually-impaired diver, followed by holding right arm up over head, swim to surface with visually-impaired diver then release hand at surface while visually-impaired diver orally inflates his buoyancy compensator.

Sensory impairment

If you have sensory impairments, you need to exercise caution during underwater swimming not to accidentally come into contact with abrasive, sharp and toxic objects, structures and marine life since you may suffer an injury without fully appreciating it. Your Adaptive Dive Team has to exercise heightened awareness of space and the surroundings as they dive with you including hazards presented by wrecks, coral heads, sea urchins, lionfish, swim-thru, lines, kelp and other aquatic life.

Exercising appropriate caution includes wearing full-length wetsuits or skins that provide adequate protection to minimize injuries and to maintain a safe swimming distance between you and potential underwater hazards. During your pre-dive briefing confirm with your Adaptive Dive Team that they know that extra precautions need to be exercised due to your sensory impairment.

Thermal Impairment

If you have thermal regulation issues, it is important for your own safety to constantly monitor this condition which can bring on hyperthermia or hypothermia during your underwater swim. It is most likely hypothermia will be the greater concern. The best precaution is to make sure you do not start your dive already cold. Wear adequate apparel prior to your dive. And of course, wear a wetsuit with thermal protection material adequate for the dive site's water temperature. Use the standard or special signals for "getting cold" to alert your dive team of your potentially hypothermic condition so they can be ready to ascend if needed.

During the pre-dive briefing you and your Adaptive Dive Team need to discuss your thermal regulation impairment and how to deal with it during your dive.

Underwater navigation

Underwater navigation depends primarily upon your ability to see the underwater terrain and your capacity to operate an underwater compass. As a practical matter, since you will be diving as a three-man dive team, you can all simply agree that one of your dive buddies will take primary responsibility for underwater navigation. Nonetheless, it is a good idea to at least know how to navigate and do it to the extent of your capabilities.

So long as your upper mobility function does not impair your capacity to manipulate the bezel on a compass and to position the lubber line in the direction you are heading, and you have vision to see the terrain, you should have the capacity to navigate underwater. Lower mobility, sensory, hearing and thermal impairments will have very little impact on this skill.

If you do have upper mobility impairments, and you have a wrist compass, try different techniques stabilizing your forearm and different levels of attachment up and down your arm. With some innovative rigging, and BCD clips, you may try to hang a console-mounted compass in a way that the lubber line is always perpendicular to your front and extends forward enough so you can see it. Even if you can't manipulate the bezel to get an accurate heading, you can at least see true north and approximate it. If desired, you can also work out a plan with your Adaptive Dive Team to use agreed upon special signals signifying that your need for assistance to operate the compass. Upon signaling, your Adaptive Dive Buddy can hold the compass so you can see it while setting the heading.

Should you have lower mobility impairments you generally should not need assistance except if you cannot stabilize yourself long enough so you can use both hands operating the compass. In this situation, you can coordinate with your Adaptive Dive Team to provide momentary assistance keeping you vertical and steady as you try to set and get a compass reading.

Another strategy you can use, depending on the terrain and assuming you can see, is to develop keener skills visually mapping out the topography of the bottom and other references to give you directional orientation.

If you are visually-impaired and do not have enough residual vision to see a compass or the terrain, underwater navigation can be accomplished thru verbal communication via a Full-Face Mask with radio transmission. Your Adaptive Dive Buddy can narrate directions and steerage to the right, left, up or down and further provide instructions directing navigation during ascents and descents and obstacle avoidance.

As with all other scuba skills, once you have determined how your Adaptive Dive Team will provide assistance for navigation, you will need to review the topic at the pre-dive briefing. Perhaps the best strategy is to reach an agreement that one dive buddy takes charge of navigation while the other serves as a backup.

As a final tip on navigation, it is prudent to have a dive team agreement that if during an open water dive, the team is uncertain of the boat's location, a pre-assigned dive buddy will momentarily ascend and surface to get a heading. A special team signal should be developed to apprise the designated diver of the need to establish the boat's location.

Mask-clearing, including removal and replacement

Mask clearing, removal and replacement are important skills for a variety of reasons. For any student diver, the skill at first is challenging but conquerable and the same is true even if you have mobility impairments. You and your instructor will determine and assess how to best perform the skill with or without assistance.

Upper mobility impairments:

If you have functional use of one arm, you should have the capacity to clear, remove and replace your mask. With practice and hard work you may be able to do these skills independently. Clearing can be accomplished using the techniques taught in your open water course -- slightly break the bottom

seal of your mask with one hand. If you do not have functional dexterity in your hands due to partial paralysis, severe spasticity, or similar dysfunction, you may need assistance. Use an agreed upon signal indicating your need for assistance, and coordinate with your dive buddy who will stabilize your head and break the bottom seal of your mask while you blow out thru your nose for mask clearance.

A certain amount of synchronization is required since you must time your exhaling with the momentary breakage of the seal. Some divers can actually master breaking the seal by applying pressure to the top frame of their mask using arm stumps. Practice different techniques and maneuvers to see if you can do this independently. If not, your adaptive team will provide the necessary assistance.

Removal and replacement of your mask is more challenging than mere mask clearing. Try different techniques to the extent your impairments allow you. Slap straps are great tools that can be used on masks to help the Adaptive Diver adjust the strap during the mask removal and replacement skill.

We have all seen some amazing You Tube footage of people with significant upper and lower mobility problems performing physical tasks that you would think not possible—like the armless mother changing her baby's diaper with her feet or someone similarly disabled playing the violin. The

point is to experiment and try different adaptations to see if you and your instructor can somehow figure out how you can best perform the skill using your own abilities.

If you and your instructor were not able to find a special technique so you can perform the skill independently, then your dive buddy will provide the required assistance. After the agreed upon signals are given communicating your need for assistance, your instructor will approach you, face to face, and give you the signal that he is removing your mask by tapping it three times. When replacing, a similar signal will be given and he will then stabilize the back of your head as he positions the mask on your face and pulls down the strap to its proper position. He will then tap your mask three times to give you the signal that he will break the seal so you can exhale through your nose to clear out the water.

Lower Mobility Impairment

Generally individuals with lower mobility impairments can perform this skill independently. Even if you have complete paraplegia or no legs, you will have the capacity to perform this skill, but you need good skills to maintain neutral buoyancy and hold a good vertical position as you perform it. Should you need assistance, the rearward buddy diver can help you maintain proper buoyancy and orientation after you give him an agreed upon signal for his assistance.

Complete Mobility Impairment

If you are an adaptive diver with complete mobility impairment (e.g. quadriplegia) and required to use a Full-Face Mask with a redundant air supply system, you will not need to remove your Full-Face Mask underwater. Clearing a Full-Face Mask is relatively easy to do. All you need to do is signal your dive buddy indicating a need for Full-Face Mask clearing and your dive buddy will push the purge button to quickly clear out the water. Most Full-Face Masks have a slightly higher positive pressure than ambient pressure reducing water leakage from occurring, and therefore, mask leakage is not a common problem.

Visual, Sensory, and Thermal Impairments- Mask clearing removal/replacement

Generally these impairments will not impede your capacity to perform these skills. If your particular impairment does for any reason, discuss and assess your need for assistance and formulate a plan to address your special needs with your Instructor and Adaptive Dive Team.

Regulator Recovery/ Retrieval

You may remove your regulator from your mouth or it may get dislodged as when another diver accidentally knocks it out. Clearly, this is a problem you must remedy in a timely manner. Your impairment may affect your ability to quickly respond. The following guidelines and adaptations are presented to help you perform this skill independently or with assistance from your team.

Upper Mobility Impairments

The nature and extent of your impairment will naturally determine if you can perform this skill independently. If you have one reasonably functioning arm that can be used to capture and replace the regulator, you should try to perform the skill. With hard work, persistent practice and adaptations, you and your instructor may find a successful formula. If your left arm is more functional, you may want to try switching the regulator to the left side low pressure port to make this easier. This will bring the regulator within reach of the better arm for retrieval.

Another very effective adaptive technique is to use a regulator necklace holder. This is a very simple rubberized necklace, that will hold the regulator within inches of your mouth should it become dislodged. If you have some limited function with either arm you may determine you can successfully replace the regulator into your mouth independently by using your impaired hands or forearms.

Complete Upper Mobility Impairment

If you have no upper mobility due to double arm amputation, quadriplegia or otherwise, you will need the assistance of your dive team. As long as you can successfully clear your regulator with your dive buddy's assistance and secure the regulator in your mouth, then you may successful perform this skill. Of course, you must accept the elevated risk of drowning, injury and death that is attendant with your inability to perform this skill independently or to perform it in a timely manner. For divers who have these impairments Diveheart strongly recommends using a Full-Face Mask to reduce risks and to enhance the margin of safety. Using a Full-Face Mask virtually eliminates the risk of losing the life support feature of conventional scuba equipment. The Full-Face Mask is firmly secured to the diver's head with several straps and the demand valve supplying air is an integral part of the unit. It is highly unlikely the Full-Face Mask will fall off the diver's head during any diving activity.

NOTE: As discussed in an earlier section, Adaptive Divers who cannot maintain a regulator in their mouth due to physical impairments will be required to use a Full-Face Mask. This Diveheart rule applies even if the diver can retrieve his own regulator.

If you cannot perform the regulator recovery independently, your Adaptive Dive Team will provide the necessary assistance. Depending on your needs, you and your dive team must discuss and plan for how and who will render assistance. Generally, this is not a difficult skill to perform for you or your dive buddies, but it is absolutely imperative that it is discussed during the Predive briefing. It is important to confirm which dive buddy will primarily monitor proper regulator placement and who will respond. It is recommended that the forward positioned dive buddy take the primary monitoring role with the understanding that both buddies should provide immediate assistance upon observing the diver without proper regulator placement.

Situational awareness is very important for all members of the dive team. The team should be mindful of the underwater environment and exercise caution around underwater structures, natural and artificial, that may catch a regulator hose and pull it out. Similarly, swimming next to a diver who uses long sweeping arm strokes presents a risk that his arm will accidently grab the other diver's hose. Being mindful and staying clear of these situations prevents accidental regulator dislodgements. Along these same lines, it is prudent to secure the regulator hose with clips keeping it close to your body or use a regulator necklace holder.

Visual Impairment

If you are blind or have other visual impairments it is likely you can perform regulator recovery independently without assistance. As with all other skills, you first must tactilely become familiar with the positions of the regulator and hose during each step of the skill. Your instructor will guide you through the skill as you practice it and will be ready to help you retrieve the regulator so you can resume breathing. Your adaptive dive team should maintain constant contact with you throughout any diving activity so you can feel assured that assistance is close by. You and your team will need to agree on a signal to alert them that you may require assistance with this skill. For instance, you may agree upon a general tactile "alert" signal where you rapidly squeeze the guiding buddy's hand so he knows to quickly respond and assess your need. If your dive buddy sees your regulator is out of your mouth, he will be ready to provide the necessary assistance if you are having trouble retrieving the regulator.

Diveheart recommends that the visually-impaired diver use the regulator necklace holder as an adaptive piece of equipment that will significantly aid the performance of this skill. Should you remove the regulator or it becomes dislodged you will always know that the regulator's position is held by the necklace only a few inches below your mouth.

Buddy-system techniques

Staying in proximity to your dive buddies is an important safety protocol for all divers regardless of their abilities. This is particularly true for adaptive scuba diving. Detailed communication during the predive briefing becomes critical when addressing potential issues underwater. If you require assistance in the water, you will have two Adaptive Dive Buddies with you at all times. An Adaptive Scuba Instructor or Advanced Adaptive Dive Buddy may be required for divers requiring a greater level of assistance. You will communicate with them, and they with you, your needs for scuba assistance, special equipment needs, diving conditions, your comfort level and other important information including depth, time and the amount of air remaining in your scuba tank. In Chapter 4 and throughout this manual you will learn about the enhance buddy system of adaptive diving and the importance of the predive briefing

Remember, for all divers, SCUBA is more enjoyable, safer and fun with your BUDDIES!

Diver Assistance Techniques & Problem Management

In your basic open water course materials, you learned how divers should assist one another with managing the following problems that may possibly occur:

- Entanglement
- Diver over exertion or fatigue
- Free flowing regulators
- Panicked Diver
- Cramp/ Spasm removal

This section will cover how to deal with these problems in the setting of adaptive diving. There is good news—these problems are quite infrequent and not likely to occur. And for Adaptive Divers the news is even better since adaptive diving involves a three member team, two of which are specially trained and certified in Adaptive Diving. This results in a greater margin of safety and more divers to assist one another. Of course it also means more buddies to share the fun and excitement of diving together.

As a general protocol all members of the team, including you must remain aware that these problems can occur and be prepared to respond to the extent of your abilities and consistent with the agreed upon dive plan. Unless otherwise agreed, should an Adaptive Dive Buddy need assistance, the other certified dive buddy should respond. You should remain ready to help. In the event you encounter any of these problems, you and your team need to discuss who and how they will be managed taking into consideration your special scuba needs.

Entanglements

Entanglements can occur even though this is an unlikely event as well. Once again, having an additional dive buddy ensures greater assistance to handle problems. In the event you become entangled, you will simply signal your dive buddies if they have not noticed the problem. In the event one of your dive buddies gets entangled, allow the other dive buddy to deal with it. Offer assistance to the extent of your abilities. Sometimes having an extra pair of hands can be useful. Regardless of your abilities, you should keep a dive knife in your possession and advise your dive buddies prior to the dive of its placement.

Diver Fatigue

Regardless of your impairment, should you become fatigued you need to alert your dive buddies using an agreed upon signal; one to let them know you are exhausted and would like to stop and rest and another to return to the boat. If you have an impairment that causes you to fatigue early than most, you must discuss this with your team and agree upon a plan to deal with physical exhaustion. The signals which you may use and the protocols for underwater and surface swimming assistance are covered in previous sections and should be followed to address this problem.

Panicked Diver at Surface

Regardless of the type of impairment you have, it is imperative that you discuss with your team any fears, anxiety or concerns you may have concerning the dive activity. During your initial training, it is not uncommon for any new diver, with or without impairments, to have some anxiety or concerns. The key is to be honest with yourself, and remain open and candid with your instructor and team members regarding any such feelings. Almost all experienced adaptive divers who had these initial feelings will tell you with practice and adequate time, you will gain the trust and confidence in yourself and your team. Practice and repeat all scuba skills until you are able to dispel those feelings, and instead perceive a comfort level that will allow you to enjoy the diving experience. This is the best preventative measure against becoming a victim of panic.

As far as your certified Adaptive Dive Buddies are concerned, it is very unlikely either one will panic in view of their special training and experience. Divers who are drawn to the adaptive diving community are typically very experienced and competent divers who are confident in their abilities to self rescue and provide assistance to other divers. Let's just say they generally have the "Right Stuff". In the very unlikely chance that one of your dive buddies does panic, the other dive buddy will respond as needed. Your responsibility would be to stay clear of the panicked diver so he does not grab you during the episode.

Free Flowing Regulators

The likelihood of a free flowing regulator becoming a problem is remote in the Adaptive Dive setting. With a three member dive team there are six functional regulators available at the start of every dive. If a regulator starts to free flow simply present the appropriate signal to share one of your dive buddy's regulators or switch over to your octopus regulator. Despite the remoteness of these occurrences, you will still learn how to breathe off of a free flowing regulator to the extent of your abilities.

Cramp/ Spasm removal

Your open water course material adequately covers how to manage cramp and muscle spasm removal. There are no special adaptive techniques for addressing this problem. However, some Adaptive Divers, due to their medical condition or impairments, may have varying degrees of muscular spasticity. If you have learned of special techniques to reduce your spasticity, share them with your team so they can provide the necessary assistance. Similarly, if your spasticity is a fairly constant condition or tends to be intermittent or varies with intensity, and represents your "normal" state and not a new onset, be sure to discuss that as well. The conversation will help your dive team appreciate what to expect and do should they observe your condition during the dive.

Basic instrument monitoring

As a diver, it is important that you monitor your depth, time and the amount of air left in your tank. You can request that information, using hand signals, or monitor your own depth and time if your mobility allows. Your Adaptive Dive Team should be able to communicate such information to you underwater by using special hand or other signals. For instance, if you are blind you will learn about special tactile signals to communicate such dive information. Tactile signals are covered in any earlier section.

You and your buddy team will be tasked with monitoring each other's gauges and who and how that will be done. Diveheart's enhanced buddy team approach adds more enjoyment and safety since everybody is watching out for each other's back, including the dive gauges—that's a pretty good system. With more trained and watchful eyes the chances of any member of the team running out of air is greatly reduced.

Underwater and surface buoyancy control

Buoyancy control makes swimming through the water easier. It also keeps you safe by helping you stay off the bottom and out of contract with sea life. On the surface, being able to establish positive buoyancy allows you to float comfortably and rest.

Your Adaptive Scuba Instructor will show you how to maintain and adjust your buoyancy if your mobility allows and will adapt the process or provide assistance as required based upon the nature and extent of your disabilities.

Whenever possible, an Adaptive Diver student should learn how to manipulate the amount of air in his BCD. There are different BCD designs that have various devices for inflation and deflation. The type and location of these devices will determine which type may best give you the opportunity to independently control your buoyancy. For instance, some inflation/deflation devices are activated by pushing a button on the end of the low pressure inflator hose while others are activated by pulling on the hose or by pushing down a lever located on the lower section of the BCD jacket. You may be able to operate some devices and others maybe too difficult due to your impairments. You and your instructor should work together to see what works best for you.

Upper Mobility Impairments

If you have upper mobility impairments, and have difficulty operating a typically left sided air inflator hose button, explore the other types of BCD that have inflation/deflation buttons, levers and pull cords located in different positions that may give you the capacity to operate them. For divers whose range of motion limitations precludes them from raising their arm above the shoulders, inflator/exhaust levers located on the bottom of a jacket may very well provide an effective adaptation. Lever devices can also be more manageable for divers who do not have much dexterity or motor control. The key is to try out different BCD devices and try different physical maneuvers to determine if you can perform this skill independently.

If you have total upper mobility impairment or no arms, you and your team will need to coordinate how to best assist your buoyancy control. More specific information regarding the procedures and protocol to adjust your buoyancy during surface and underwater swimming and controlled ascents/descents are discussed in other sections of this manual.

Visual Impairments

Buoyancy control is partially a function of your capacity to see your position in the water column. It much easier to know whether you are sinking deeper or floating upwards if you can see the bottom or the surface. Those points of reference enable you to figure out whether you need to add or dump air. Moreover, with impaired vision you would not have the benefit of

watching your depth gauge or monitor your computer's rate of descent/ascents. For those reasons, you will need some assistance to maintain and control your buoyancy. Special tactile signals to communicate the need to adjust buoyancy by adding or dumping air and special dive team protocols designed to assist you in maintaining safe ascent/descent rates are discussed in other sections of this manual.

One special adaptation tool visually-impaired divers can use is to always activate the audible alarms indicating unsafe ascent rates.

Impairments --Lower Mobility, Hearing, Sensory and Thermal

Impairments that affect lower mobility, hearing, sensory or thermal will not generally affect a diver's capacity to control his own buoyancy.

Special Consideration for Mobility-impaired divers

Since there is a greater chance that a mobility-impaired diver may lose their proper swimming or surface orientation and find that their head is below a horizontal position, it is important that during training mobility-impaired divers practice how to dump air from the lower segments of their BCD. Most

BCD's have pull cord styled dump valves that can be activated when the diver is in a downward position.

Controlled Descents and Ascents

Slow controlled descents and ascents are imperative. Because there is an elevated risk of barotrauma and decompression sickness for someone who cannot independently control the rate of descent / ascent, or maintain neutral buoyancy for safety or decompression stops, the support team must control their own buoyancy and provide necessary AND TIMELY assistance to you.

The three member dive team (i.e., Adaptive Diver, Adaptive Dive Buddies or Advanced Adaptive Dive Buddies) must perform a multitude of skills to safely and efficiently execute controlled ascents/descents. This involves multitasking and requires the team to coordinate with each other the following tasks:

- Communicating with all members of the team by developing clear signaling
- Controlling your buoyancy by inflating and deflating your BCD
- Synchronize the rate of ascent/descent with the dive team

- Synchronized hovering with the entire team
- Monitoring whether you require assistance with equalization and signaling the need to stop, ascend or descend for equalization
- Monitoring your gauges
- Alternate air supply procedure in the event of an out-of-air emergency
- Use of the descent line

Descents

The first step is for the entire team to properly position themselves at the surface next to the descent line. At the start of the descent, the Adaptive Dive Buddy providing assistance with communication/signaling will be positioned in front, face to face with you while the other Adaptive Dive Buddy assisting with inflating/deflating your BCD will be positioned behind and slightly to the left so he can easily reach the BCD low pressure inflator buttons or levers. The same Adaptive Dive Buddy will tether himself to the descent line by wrapping his leg around the descent line while holding onto your tank valve with his hand and using his knees to keep you vertical.

Safety Alert: If you are using a Full-Face Mask, double check to make sure the tank valve is on and that the air vent valve has been closed.

One Adaptive Dive Buddy will be in constant contact with you while the other Adaptive Dive Buddy makes only incidental contact. After the descent signal is given, it is essential that each diver first establish neutral buoyancy at the surface and then, with breath control or a very small increment of deflation, descend no more than a couple of feet (a meter) below the surface and hover. The forward positioned Adaptive Dive Buddy should try to minimize contact with you that could alter your neutral buoyancy the rearward Adaptive Dive Buddy is trying to establish.

Once neutral buoyancy is established at three feet, the forward Adaptive Dive Buddy will signal to determine if you are comfortable and OK, and most importantly look for any signs or signals that there is an equalization problem. Once you have signaled OK, the forward Adaptive Dive Buddy will give an OK signal coupled with a descent signal to proceed with a very slow descent.

As a team, you will stop every 3-4 feet/one meter so the forward Adaptive Dive Buddy can confirm effective equalization with you. If there is a problem, the rearward Adaptive Dive Buddy will stop the descent and ascend a couple of feet/one meter. The rearward Adaptive Dive Buddy must carefully observe this process. It is not uncommon for an Adaptive Diver to need a much longer time to equalize, especially when using a Full-Face Mask.

If the rearward Adaptive Dive Buddy becomes distracted for any reason, such as becoming preoccupied with adjusting his own equipment, the forward Adaptive Dive Buddy must step in and take control of assisting the Adaptive Diver's buoyancy and rate of descent.

Ascents

The protocol for the ascent is essentially the same as for the descents, although use of the descent line may not be as necessary. Certainly if the descent line is available, you should use it.

You should follow a very conservative ascent rate and safety stop protocol. It is Diveheart's philosophy and practice to follow very conservative dive profiles, including extra conservative ascent rates for all dives. It is recommended that the ascent rate not exceed 30 feet/10 meters per minute regardless of depth and to always make a three minute safety stop at 15 feet/five meters.

Equalization

Timely and effective equalization is vital to avoid the injuries and complications related to barotraumas. Accordingly, it is critical that the dive team communicate and coordinate their assistance in helping you equalize.

The Adaptive Dive Buddy providing primary assistance with equalization will monitor your needs by maintaining continuous and direct eye contact with you. If for any reason the Adaptive Dive Buddy responsible for equalization must break direct supervision, he will signal to the other Adaptive Dive Buddy that he is now providing primary assistance with equalization.

Being familiar with the equalization features of your mask or Full-Face Mask, is essential to knowing how to perform effective equalization. The following protocol should be observed:

Prior to the dive both Adaptive Dive Buddies must be familiar with the nose configuration of the Adaptive Diver's mask and how your nose seats within the mask or Full-Face Mask and both should practice whether a valsalva equalization can be performed. A trial run, before entering the water, should be performed with you wearing the Full-Face Mask so your Adaptive Diver Buddy knows exactly how to position his fingers within the nose piece or Full-Face Mask to apply pressure to close off your nostrils. It's not uncommon that the assisting Adaptive Dive Buddy squeezes too close to the nostrils falsely believing he is effectively assisting with the valsalva, when in reality he is only pinching nose cartilage.

Similarly, predive practice with the Full-Face Mask will test whether the nostril blocking devices or parts are adjusted and seated properly for nasal airway blockage. This should be done well in advance of the dive so you can check to make sure you have the necessary tools, if any, for adjustments or swapping out nasal pieces. Failure to do this can ruin a perfectly beautiful dive day. You and the Adaptive Dive Buddy primarily assisting with equalization must take steps to make sure this is done.

If Valsalva fails, the Adaptive Dive Buddy should have special signals for reminding you to try other techniques such as side to side jaw manipulations, or open mouth, as well as ear tugging techniques. Mimicking signals should be adequate, but it's important to review such special signals during the predive briefing.

During the predive briefing the Adaptive Dive Buddies should discuss with you whether you typically equalize easily and quickly or whether you require more than average time to properly equalize. Also, the dive team should review which equalization techniques work best for you so the Adaptive Dive Buddy providing assistance will know which technique to administer first.

The Adaptive Dive Buddy primarily responsible for equalization must communicate/signal with the other buddy assisting with buoyancy control to adjust depths, or hover for equalization.

Monitoring for mask squeezes is no different, except that such squeezes generally occur during the early part of the dive and are not easily resolved by most underwater clearing techniques. The dive team must consider aborting the dive until there is resolution of nasal airway blockage.

Use descent lines when possible or desirable. It is a very good tool in maintaining a constant depth for hovering or to make precise 2-3ft adjustments in depth to facilitate equalization maneuvers.

Cover all aspects of equalization and how it will be performed during the Predive briefing, who is primarily providing assistance and how the Adaptive Dive Buddy will coordinate their efforts as outlined above.

The Adaptive Dive Buddy team should practice special signals so, if the Valsalva maneuver fails, they can remind you to try other techniques as discussed above. It is important to review these special signals during the predive briefing.

Out-of-air emergencies

Learning and maintaining skills to manage out-of-air emergencies is clearly important for any diver, and especially critical for Adaptive Divers who cannot independently perform them.

Although it is essential that you and your dive team receive training so everybody can be prepared for serious events, out-of-air emergencies are very unlikely in Adaptive Dive Team diving. With two specially trained Adaptive Dive Buddies, you receive the benefit of redundancy. Not only does the Diveheart Adaptive Dive Buddy system mandate that two Adaptive Dive Buddies stay close and provide assistance, it also requires more experienced and trained Advanced Adaptive Dive Buddies for Adaptive Divers requiring assistance with out-of-air emergencies.

The enhanced buddy system also eliminates any need for you to undergo special training in Controlled Emergency Swimming Ascents or emergency buoyant ascents since it is very probable that at least one Adaptive Dive Buddy will have an adequate air supply for alternate air sharing—a benefit that is enjoyed by all members of the team.

The focus on assisting with out-of-air emergencies will be on how the team manages and coordinates alternative air source sharing using octopus regulators, Full-Face Masks with bailout procedures, and Full-Face Masks with special alternate or redundant air supply systems (i.e., pony tanks).

Alternate air source sharing

Sharing an alternate air source regulator (i.e., octopus) with any member of the team can be challenging if none of the divers have prepared for it. Since out-of-air emergencies typically occur at depth, all of the skills related to controlled ascents, equalization and Full-Face Mask use will come to bear—a significant "task loading" event. Practicing and following the below described protocols will best prepare all concerned and substantially mitigate the risk associated with such situations.

Assistance for Full-Face Mask Use

The Full-Face Mask should be used for Adaptive Divers whose disability makes it difficult for them to breathe safely underwater using a standard regulator or if there is a need to communicate verbally because physical signaling is not possible or effective.

The Adaptive Scuba Instructor will assess whether you require a Full-Face Mask during training and that requirement will be placed on your certification card. The following factors and questions should be considered:

Does your disability preclude you from securing and maintaining proper placement of the second stage regulator in his mouth during a dive?

Traumatic injuries or other medical conditions may impair your capacity to bite down or hold a regulator in place. A traumatic injury may have injured a facial or cranial nerve that controls the jaw muscles responsible for securing a regulator, or you may have some type of neuromuscular disorder that causes mouth/jaw muscle spasticity or weakness that may place you at risk for spitting out the regulator or preventing an adequate mouth seal. Either situation could place you at risk of drowning.

You and your Adaptive Dive Team will have to determine if a Full-Face Mask can effectively address these problems and reduce the risk. If so, the Full-Face Mask will be required.

Do you have a physical disability that precludes you from effectively communicating underwater using hand signals or other physical signals?

Due to severe disabilities involving arm or leg movements, such as with complete quadriplegia, severe spasticity, or multiple amputations, it may be virtually impossible for you to communicate effectively using hand or other physical signals. With the exception of nods of the head or eye blinking, there may be no other way to communicate by signaling. In these cases, the use of a Full-Face Mask with electronic communication is clearly the best option and is recommended equipment for such divers.

Do you have a cognitive impairment that precludes you from communicating effectively underwater with hand signals or will U/W communications give you needed emotional support ?

Some Adaptive Divers with cognitive impairments have difficulty communicating clearly with hand signals. For others, such as some autistic individuals, verbal communication may be necessary. You may need to hear a familiar and trusted voice to help reduce emotional stressors. A Full-Face Mask with electronic communication can also be helpful for persons with other cognitive impairments where remembering and comprehending what the signals mean is difficult. In these cases, a Full-Face Mask with electronic communications should be considered.

Safety Alert: **If underwater verbal communications are necessary to perform any of the key scuba skills effectively, such equipment is mandatory.**

If you answered yes to any of the above questions, you should carefully consider the use of a Full-Face Mask, and should further consider whether electronic communication is necessary. Your adaptive scuba instructor will make recommendations and/or decide whether you are required to use one.

Special considerations for Full-Face Mask selection

- Proper fit
- Effective nasal blocking
- Alternative air capability without Full-Face Mask removal (redundant air supply valve)
- Capacity to bail out of Full-Face Mask and use regulator second stage.

There are a number of Full-Face Mask brands and models available. The Advanced Adaptive Dive Buddy or Adaptive Scuba Instructor should have basic knowledge regarding what special features would best meet your special scuba needs.

Proper Fit: Selecting a Full-Face Mask that fits properly is essential, as with any mask. Some brands/models come in different sizes and some are one-size-fits-all. It is important that the fit is comfortable and does not cause any sensitivities. Checking for a good seal from the top and side of the skirt is important to avoid air leakage and air supply depletion.

Be sure to read the owner's manual to know the recommended procedure for donning and fitting the Full-Face Mask. Virtually all manufacturers have posted their manuals on the internet and provide online  demonstration videos. There are several YouTube demonstration videos, as well. It is strongly recommended that you review the videos and manuals that relate to the specific brand and model of the Full-Face Mask being used.

Effective nasal blocking: Proper fitting also includes making sure the Full-Face Mask parts or devices used for the Valsalva maneuver are adjusted and/or available. The owner's manual provides the technical information for changing parts or making adjustments. For instance the Ocean Reef Neptune model has nose buds of different sizes and shapes designed to block the nasal airways for equalization. You will need to become familiar with how to make those adjustments until a proper fit is achieved.

Redundant and/or Alternate air supply capabilities: For safety reasons, it is important to select a Full-Face Mask that has redundant and/or alternate air supply capabilities for Adaptive Divers who cannot perform a Full-Face Mask bailout in the event of an out-of-air emergency or demand valve malfunction.

For example, if your disability prevents you from keeping a regulator second stage in your mouth securely, due to mouth spasticity or jaw muscle weakness, you will not be able to bail out and use an Adaptive Dive Buddy's octopus regulator. You will need to select a Full-Face Mask that has the capacity to quickly connect to an alternate air supply such as a pony tank, or from an Adaptive Dive Buddy's tank by using a spare low pressure hose with a female quick release connector to the male counterpart on the Full-Face Mask. The Ocean Reef Full-Face Mask has those features.

UW Electronic Communications

Due to severe disabilities involving arm or leg movements, such as with complete quadriplegics, severe spasticity, or multiple amputees, it may be virtually impossible for the Adaptive Diver to effectively communicate using hand or other physical signals .With the exception of nods of the head or eye blinking, there may be no other way to communicate by signaling. With such divers, using a Full-Face Mask with electronic communication is clearly the best option and is recommended.

Additionally, some Adaptive Divers with cognitive impairments may have difficulty communicating clearly with hand signals or there may not be a way to grab their attention unless verbal communications were possible. For instance an autistic Adaptive Diver may need some verbal prompting to get their attention to respond to hand signals. Some Adaptive Divers may need to hear a familiar and trusted to voice before they will engage in responding, or to help reduce emotional stressors. Full-Face Mask with electronic communication can also be helpful with other cognitive dysfunctions where remembering and comprehending what the signals mean or how they will be given are impaired. For these Adaptive Divers, Full-Face Mask with electronic communication "may" be required.

Predive briefing regarding the Full-Face Mask

During the predive briefing, all aspects of Full-Face Mask use must be addressed, including the following:
- Is the most appropriate and necessary Full-Face Mask available, and are all accessory items, including tools, present and operational, (e.g., electronic transmission devices, redundant air supply valve, extra low pressure hoses with quick releases, pony tanks, batteries)?

- Which Advanced Adaptive Dive Buddy will provide primary assistance regarding assembly, testing, fitting, adjusting and storing the Full-Face Mask?
- Which Adaptive Dive Buddy will be primarily responsible for opening the tank valve and opening and closing the Full-Face Mask vent? (See Safety Alert regarding air vent management below)
- Which Advanced Adaptive Dive Buddy will provide primary assistance with underwater equalization, Full-Face Mask adjustments and monitoring?

Since each Full-Face Mask is designed differently, all dive support team members MUST review equalization techniques so every member of the team is familiar with how the mask operates.

Discuss any and all special signals that relate to Full-Face Mask use, regardless of whether electronic communication is used, since signals may become necessary should the electronic device fail.

Discuss the procedure for an out-of-air emergency. If a Full-Face Mask bailout is a possibility, or if you may have to use an alternate air supply with direct connects to the Full-Face Mask, decide who will assist with converting to the alternative or redundant air supply; the hook ups, turning on valves, etc.

After the predive briefing but prior to the dive you and your team must test whether you can effectively perform the Valsalva maneuver. You must don the Full-Face Mask with the air vent open and both members of the support team must test whether they are correctly assisting you with the Valsalva maneuver.

Special signals when electronic underwater communication unavailable

In the event a Full-Face Mask with electronic communications is not available and you cannot physically signal using upper extremities, you and the dive support team will have to develop special signals, where you signaling back with a "Yes" or "No" signal either by nodding or eye blinking. During the predive briefing it is essential that all members of the dive team fully understand what the special signals are and how they will be given as well as how you will respond. You should practice the signals during the predive briefing.

There is no set standard for special signals. The following are examples that could be incorporated into the dive plan and briefing relative to NSA with Full-Face Mask:

Breathing from Full-Face Mask is <u>NOT</u> OK: Adaptive Dive Buddy moves right hand to chest and motions in and out (signaling respirations) and then presents OK signal for you to respond accordingly. If hand signals are possible you will display the out-of-air sign. If hand signals are not possible, you will signal NO with rapid and continuous nods or eye blinks.

Checking Straps: Adaptive Dive Buddy will present stop and hover signals and then point to Full-Face Mask and present stretching motion with the fingers of both hands as though stretching a rubber band between them. You should respond with OK signal.

Requesting check for leaks: You request a check on face mask straps to check for leaks or tightness. You present three "No" shakes of the head with a prolonged pause at least 15 seconds before repeating signal.

Time to end the dive: You alternate nods of the head from "yes to no" until Adaptive Dive Buddy presents OK signal to confirm that dive will be ended.

Safety Alert: Adaptive Divers who are not capable of independently opening the air vent are at an elevated risk of suffocating if the air vent and the tank valve are closed or the tank is empty.

Air Vent Management

It is mandatory to comply with the following procedure regarding air vent management:

- When you are ready to don scuba gear, your Adaptive Dive Buddy must make sure the tank valve is turned on and the Full-Face Mask air vent valve is open.
- After the Full-Face Mask is fitted and strapped creating a proper seal, close the air vent and test the entire system. The air vent valve should remain closed throughout the dive.
- Upon surfacing, and as long as the tank has sufficient air supply (i.e. no less than 500psi), your dive buddies will keep the air vent valve closed until it is time to remove your gear or you are getting close to air depletion.. At that time, they can open the air vent and detach the Full-Face Mask if the unit has a quick release. This

- makes it easier to remove the rest of the gear for the boat transfer.
- If the Full-Face Mask unit does not have a quick release, then your Adaptive Dive Buddy team will remove your Full-Face Mask while you are floating on your back. Then they will remove the rest of the scuba gear for transfer back to the boat or pool's edge. In both situations, everyone should have their BCDs sufficiently inflated to maintain your head above water.
- If you surface with no air supply, or run out of air while waiting to exit the water, the Advanced Adaptive Dive Buddy with primary responsibility to assist with Full-Face Mask should open the air vent immediately.

Out-of-air Adaptive Diver with standard mask and regulator

- Adaptive Diver gives out-of-air signal
- Adaptive Dive Buddy gives octopus to Adaptive Diver
- If the primary Adaptive Dive Buddy does not immediately respond to the Adaptive Diver then the secondary Adaptive Dive Buddy will immediately provide his octopus to the Adaptive Diver.
- Primary Adaptive Dive Buddy signals other Adaptive Dive Buddy so that other Adaptive Dive Buddy is aware of alternate air sharing.
- Ascent: Primary Adaptive Dive Buddy assisting with communications takes forward position and rearward Adaptive Dive Buddy assisting with controlled ascent gets ready to take control of his and the Adaptive Diver's BCD inflation/deflation buttons or dump valves.
- Rearward Adaptive Dive Buddy signals to start ascent.
- Ascent is performed at no more than 30 feet/10 meters per minute and three minute safety stop is executed at 15 feet if available air supply is sufficient for both divers sharing air.
- Immediately upon surfacing, forward Adaptive Dive Buddy inflates his BCD for surface buoyancy and assist adaptive diver with surface buoyancy.

- Rearward Adaptive Dive Buddy establishes positive surface buoyancy for himself and manually inflates the Adaptive Diver's BCD.
- Adaptive Diver replaces regulator with his snorkel with either Adaptive Dive Buddy's assistance.

Out-of-air emergencies with Full-Face Mask bail-out capable Adaptive Diver

Note: "Bailout-capable Adaptive Diver" means an Adaptive Diver who has the ability to secure and safely breathe off of a standard regulator second stage without a mask.

- Adaptive Diver gives out-of-air signal
- Primary/ forward Adaptive Dive Buddy assists the Adaptive Diver with removing his Full-Face Mask.
- Rearward Adaptive Dive Buddy detaches his octopus rig and hands it to Adaptive Diver or assist Adaptive diver in placement of mouth piece to restore AD's U/W breathing depending on the diver's abilities.
- The primary/ forward Adaptive Dive Buddy assists the Adaptive Diver in purging excess water from the octopus, if necessary and the Adaptive Diver breathes from the octopus.
- The primary /forward Adaptive Dive Buddy removes the backup standard mask and assists the Adaptive Diver with putting it on and clearing the mask.
- Ascent: Adaptive Dive Buddy with primary communications and equalization responsibilities takes forward position and rearward Adaptive Dive Buddy takes control of his and the Adaptive Diver's BCD inflation/deflation buttons or dump valves.
- Rearward Adaptive Dive Buddy signals to start ascent and proceeds with controlled ascent, 30 feet/10 meters per minute and executes safety stop if available air supply is sufficient for both divers sharing air.
- Immediately upon surfacing the forward Adaptive Dive Buddy inflates his BCD for surface buoyancy while the rearward

Adaptive Dive Buddy establishes positive surface buoyancy for himself and manually inflates the Adaptive Diver's BCD.

- The Adaptive Diver replaces the regulator with his snorkel with either Adaptive Dive Buddy's assistance.

Out-of-air emergencies for Adaptive Divers not capable of Full-Face Mask bailouts

New technology originally designed for industrial, military and police diving activities, to enhance safety is also perfectly suitable and adds safety for Adaptive Divers who require a Full-Face Mask. A device manufactured by Sartek Industries, called a Redundant Supply Valve (RSV), eliminates the elevated risk associated with Full-Face Mask bailouts. With the RSV attached to the Full-Face Mask and a pony tank, the Adaptive Diver or his Dive Buddy can easily switch over to the redundant air supply of the pony tank without ever having to remove the Full-Face Mask underwater.

In an out-of-air emergency, the primary Adaptive Dive Buddy simply slides a switch to convert over to the reserve air pony tank to provide air to the Adaptive Diver. Once done, the dive team merely completes a controlled ascent. On the surface, leave the Full-Face Mask on the Adaptive Diver with air vent valve open.

Because the RSV eliminates the associated risk with bailouts and relieves the dive team of related task-loaded procedures, Diveheart recommends RSV use for all Full-Face Mask adaptive diving. Adaptive Divers who cannot proficiently or safely perform a bailout procedure will be required to use a FFM with a redundant supply valve. (See mandatory FFM rules). An alternative to the Redundant Supply Valve application in out-of-air emergencies is using a Full-Face Mask equipped with a male quick release connector. By attaching an extra low pressure hose with a female quick release connector to the Adaptive Dive Buddy's regulator first stage, an out-of-air emergency can be easily resolved. All the Adaptive Dive Buddy needs to do is attach his extra low pressure hose to the Full-Face Mask male quick release connector.

After the dive team establishes buoyancy at the surface, the primary Adaptive Dive Buddy should open the air vent on the Full-Face Mask and then disconnect the alternate low pressure hose from the Full-Face Mask.

If you plan to use this out-of-air method, test the equipment to confirm that the quick connects and release mechanisms operate effectively. If this proves to be technically difficult or does not work, then the procedure obviously SHOULD NOT BE USED.

Note: Connecting the alternate low pressure hose underwater may introduce water into the second stage creating the need for greater servicing of the Full-Face Mask demand valve. The need to practice the skill periodically will undoubtedly generate greater maintenance cost and also increase the risk of regulator malfunction.

Descents lines for Key Scuba Skills

For Adaptive Divers requiring assistance with controlled ascents/descents, Full-Face Mask use, equalization, or who may otherwise require more time to descend, using a descent line with a buoy and anchor adds a margin of safety and is recommended.

The best practice for using the descent line is to have the rearward positioned Adaptive Dive Buddy with responsibility to assist the Adaptive Diver with a controlled descent to wrap his leg around the descent line while receiving and responding to the hand signals from the Adaptive Diver or the other Adaptive Dive Buddy to level, ascend or descend.

From a dive boat, the descent line or lines should be directly attached to the floating current line off the back of the boat.

While secured to the line with the leg wrap technique, your dive buddy's hands will be freed up to manipulate the buttons, valves and lever used for BCD inflation and purging, for him and you, as well as, for equalization and signaling.

The descent line is recommended regardless of whether a current is initially present since currents are unpredictable and can develop within a short time and change directions without notice.

During training and other diving activities, the descent line also serves as a visual reference to help you and your dive team gauge ascent rates and is especially useful to help the team maintain the same depth during safety stops.

CHAPTER 6: ADAPTIVE EQUIPMENT

Thanks to the wide variety of existing traditional scuba gear and existing specialty scuba gear, the vast majority of individuals with disabilities are able to experience zero gravity underwater even if it's just in a swimming pool. *It is important to note that there is very little gear that is specially designed for Adaptive Diving since existing gear can do the job for the vast majority of Adaptive Divers.* Regardless of their abilities, most adaptive divers will be on more equal terms underwater just because of the forgiving nature of zero gravity.

Traditional scuba gear is more suitable for certain adaptive divers based on their abilities and needs. For example, a weight-integrated Buoyancy Compensation Device (BCD) with a variety of D rings is appropriate for a diver who cannot accommodate a weight belt because of atrophied lower extremities. Accompanied with a set of traditional ankle weights, such mobility-impaired divers are able to dive without any special modifications to traditional gear.

With Diveheart Adaptive Scuba Training and well-trained adaptive dive buddies and instructors, many individuals with disabilities can also experience life-changing scuba adventure dives around the world. This chapter identifies some of the existing equipment that can be used by an individual with a disability so that they can enjoy the freedom and exhilaration that comes with scuba diving.

Conventional Equipment Used for Adaptive Diving:
- Standard Face mask
- Prescription/Magnification Mask
- Full-Face Mask
- Full-Face Mask with Communications
- Scuba Fins(of varying weights & configurations)
- Webbed gloves
- Prosthetic Fins
- Buoyancy Compensation Devices
- Weighting
- Wet Suits
- Dry Suits
- Transfer Gear & Equipment
- Protective Matting
- Belts and Lashes
- Beach Wheelchairs
- Descent lines with buoy and anchor
- Regulator Necklace Holder
- Adaptive Diver Profile Slate

Standard Face mask

The scuba mask encloses the eyes and nose. Traditional scuba training will show you how to care for the mask, defog the mask, clear the mask and more. Most masks are pretty standard; however, it is important that your mask conforms to your face. Some masks have purge valves below the nose. This is a special feature that helps divers clear water out of the mask easily. By simply tilting your head forward, you can easily clear water from your mask by just blowing through their nose. This is great for divers who may not be able to hold the mask against their face while clearing.

Some purge masks however make it harder to equalize your ears since they lack the nose pinching features necessary to perform a valsalva maneuver. There are a variety of masks with purge valves on the market. Make sure you select the mask that is most appropriate for you.

There are a variety of masks with purge valves on the market. Make sure you select the mask that is most appropriate for you.

Prescription/Magnification Mask

Some Visually-impaired divers who are nearsighted can benefit from a Prescription/Magnification mask allowing them to see better while diving without their glasses or contacts.

Full-Face Mask

Divers who have trouble maintaining a regulator in their mouths or are incapable of independently recovering and clearing their regulator are required to use a Full-Face Mask. For such divers a full-face mask essentially eliminates the risk of drowning that would otherwise be present due to their lack of ability to independently maintain placement or retrieve and breathe from their regulator.

There are several types of Full-Face Mask with similar features. The quick release on the Ocean Reef Full-Face Mask allows the Adaptive Buddy Dive team to completely remove the scuba unit while leaving the Full-Face Mask on the Adaptive Diver while bringing the diver to the boat after a dive. This feature provides constant protection of the airway during the transfer back onto the boat.

You will have to have special training in how to use the mask, how to equalize, how to bail out from the mask in an emergency and accept a regulator or activate the redundant air supply valve. All of these topics are covered in other sections of this manual and your instructor will provide further training in its use.

Full-Face Mask with Communications

Some Full-Face Masks include built-in communication devices that allow divers to talk underwater. This makes diving safer and more fun for Visually-impaired drivers.

It makes the dive experience more socially rewarding as their dive buddy carries on conversations providing real time narrations of the underwater scenes.

For divers who have cognitive, emotional or, psychological impairments, where verbal communications can help reduce anxiety or promote more effective communications, the full face mask may prove to be an important piece of adaptive equipment. Your adaptive scuba instructor can help you decide whether a FFM would be appropriate for you.

Scuba Fins

Traditional scuba foot fins are another tool that can be used to enhance the Adaptive Diver's experience. Some divers who have limited or no use of their legs wear full foot or open-heel fins so they feel more like a diver. It also gives them an opportunity to use their abilities to develop underwater mobility and to develop their musculature.

From a weighting perspective, fins may add needed weight or trim to the mobility-impaired diver and may help the Adaptive Dive team to navigate the Adaptive Diver through the water. Fins can become a detriment, however, if there is current as the water pressure catches the fins and makes u/w swimming more challenging.

Some Adaptive Divers use a monofin designed for freediving. This allows the Adaptive Diver to put both feet or stubs into one single fin. For some divers, this type of fin generates more u/w thrust and efficiently utilizes the mobility and power of both legs. Some divers who have the ability to torque their body in the water also can use a monofin despite the inability to use their legs. These fins can also be specially adapted to accommodate the adaptive diver's unique needs.

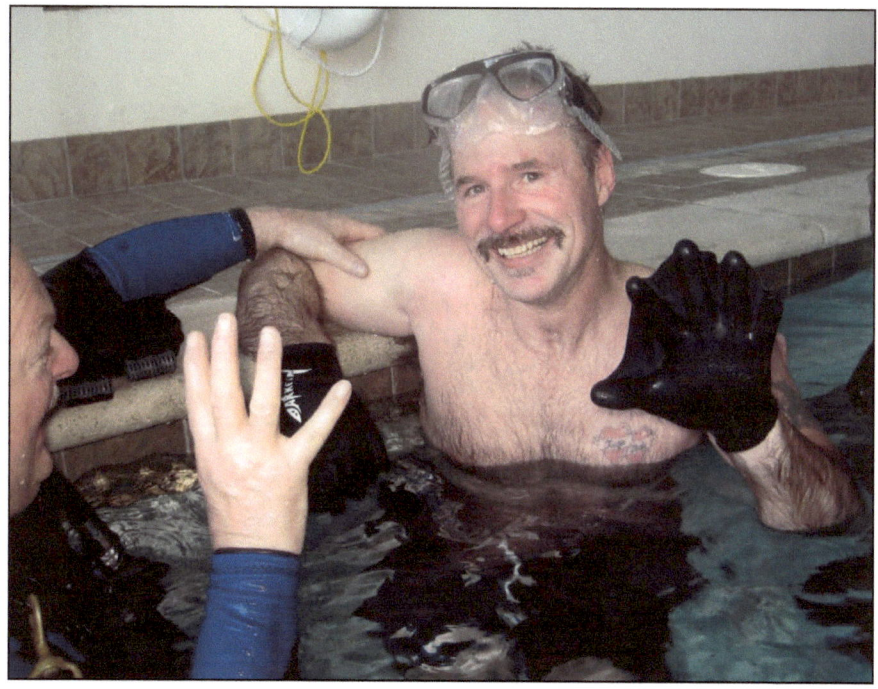

Webbed gloves

When foot fins are not an option, Adaptive Divers can use hand fins, webbed gloves, or arm prosthetics so that they can propel themselves through the water. One thing to look for is a glove that gives dexterity with your fingers so you can manipulate your equipment. Some webbed gloves have no finger tips for this reason. Other webbed gloves like Darkfin articulate the fingers placing the webbing over the top of the fingers. This feature allows you to manipulate equipment effectively. Ideally select a glove that fits, is comfortable and effectively propels you thru the water, while at the same time gives you sufficient dexterity to give hand signal and manipulate the various buttons and levers of your gear

Prosthetic Fins

Amputees with a prosthetic swim leg with an adjustable foot can be outfitted with a fin so that diver can more effectively swim. Another benefit of prosthetic fin is that the diver will be more symmetrical making special weight trimming unnecessary. Prosthetics also have an aesthetic benefit which is emotionally pleasing for some divers. .

Buoyancy Compensation Devices

Proper buoyancy in scuba diving is critical and there are many tools that we can use to help divers of all abilities achieve neutral buoyancy. One of the traditional pieces of equipment is the Buoyancy Compensation Device (BCD). Diveheart has learned that a jacket-style weight-integrated BCD with a variety of D rings work best with Adaptive Divers for a variety of reasons. The D rings allow the Adaptive Diver to add incremental weight to the BCD for trimming.

Back inflation BCDs tend to push the Adaptive Diver forward or face first in the water making it more difficult if not impossible for an Adaptive Diver to safely turn over in the water. For this reason Diveheart discourages the use of back inflation BCDs for Adaptive Divers.

Divers with upper mobility impairments may find that BCDs with special intergrated regulators and power inflator are easier to use because of where the buttons and deflator mechinism are located. For example such combine devices have inflator buttons next to the second stage regulator and dumping air can be achieved by pulling on the hose dowardly eliminating the need to raise your inflator hose above your head. Some BCDs include levers instead of the conventional buttons at the end of the inflator hose which some divers find easier to operate.

A final consideration is the amount of lift that a BCD has. This is especially important when a diver is obese or is particularly negatively buoyant at the surface.

Weighting

The Weight Harness is another great tool for individuals who have atrophied lower extremities, amputations or those who are challenged by obesity issues. A Weight harnesses is a good option to consider when a traditional weight belt or integrated BCD cannot hold enough weight to trim out the adaptive or obese diver. A harness is also useful for the mobility impaired diver who has an atrophied waist line and/or buttocks allowing a weight belt to slip off.

Clip on and ankle weights give the adaptive diver the option of a variety of weighting scenarios. Numerous D rings on the BCD provide opportunities for the Adaptive Diver to experiment with a variety of ways to trimmed out weighting for neutral buoyancy, and underwater and surface swimming.

Wet Suits

Thermal regulation can be a problem for an Adaptive Diver, who has a spinal cord injury or other neuromuscular disorder where thermal regulation is compromised. Wet suits are designed to keep warmer water, heated by the body, up against the skin while it provides thermal protection from colder water outside the wetsuit. Custom wetsuits with zippers and gussets make it more convenient for Adaptive Divers to don the wetsuit. Sometimes it takes more than one Adaptive Dive Buddy to assist the Adaptive Diver don their wetsuit. Wetsuits with long with zippers and gussets make the process easier.

Wetsuits are also easier to put on if you first don a dive skin. Some suits have a special lining inside the suit for easy donning. There are also warming devices on the market that can be placed in certain areas of the wetsuit to keep you warm. They are very similar to the soft warming packs used by snow skiers but are made for underwater use. New battery powered thermal wetsuits have also reached the shelves of dive shops which are quite effective in providing warmth for divers vulnerable to hypothermia. The extent and nature of your thermal regulation impairment should determine what type of suite will best serve your needs.

Dry Suits

Dry suits are another tool that most divers are aware of, but may not be familiar using. Dry suits can be a welcome piece of equipment for an

Adaptive Diver who has thermal regulation issues since the diver stays dry, except for the face and hands.

One of the challenges when using a dry suit is to effectively control buoyancy. Your Adaptive Dive Buddy team would need to be comfortable and competent with dry suits themselves before diving with you. You will have to learn all the special techniques that come along with diving with a dry suit. There are a variety of dry suit courses that are offered by dry suit manufacturers and scuba training agencies.

Transfer Gear & Equipment

You are fully aware of your transfer needs on land before entering the dive scene and can greatly assist your Adaptive Dive Buddy team as they plan transfers onto and off of a dive boat or to and from a dive site on shore. One device you can use to make transfers and dive experiences more safe and fun is the Transfer Harness. Most of the world is not wheelchair accessible and many times an Adaptive Diver must be carried from their wheelchair to the boat or manually transferred to and from the boat and dock. The multi-handled Transfer Harness allows many Adaptive Dive Buddies or support staff to take part in the transfer.

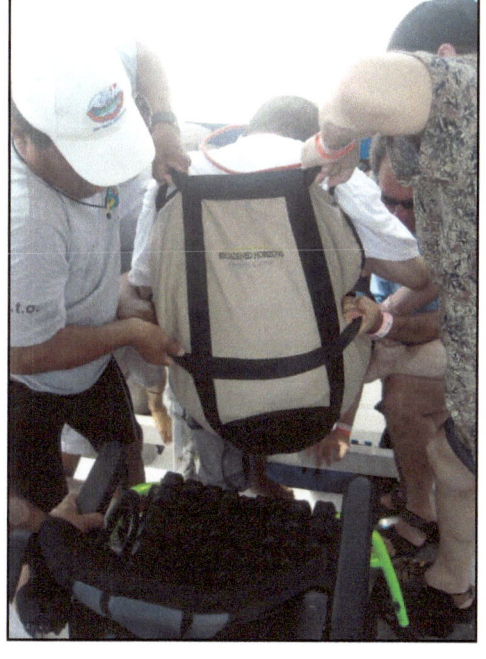

Adaptive divers who usually use power chairs on land will not be able to bring those chairs on the vast majority of dive boats, nor should such expensive equipment be exposed to marine and other wet environments. Light weight manual wheel chairs are more suitable for dive boats and navigating around dockage and other dive related activities. .

Protective Matting

If you are susceptible to skin break down or pressure sores, you should bring a protective matt to any diving related activity to avoid such problems. Pool side accommodations and dive boat seating is typically hard and uncushioned. Your susceptibility to skin breakdown will decide how much padding you may require. There are lots of protective pads on the market. Find one that provides adequate protection given your weight, how much subcutaneous fat you have and its ability to cushion your skin. The material should be light weight and foldable. Look for mats and pads that can tolerate wet environments and have a non-slip characteristic so it does not present a slip hazard.

Belts and Lashes

When seas are even a little rough, a wheelchair is susceptible to unwanted movement while on a rocking boat so securing it to a fixed object like a pole adds another level of comfort and security for the Adaptive Diver who uses a wheelchair. Blank weight belts or gate belts can be used for this purpose.

Adaptive divers who are unable to use their legs for underwater mobility may use neoprene straps with Velcro™ to secure their legs together during the dive. Some straps also have a handle on them so that the Adaptive Dive Buddy can use the handle to better manage the adaptive diver underwater. An Adaptive Diver may find these items handy when trying to manage their lower extremities during the dive.

Beach Wheelchairs

Balloon tire beach wheelchairs can make long traverses across sand during a shore dive much more efficient and safe.

Underwater Propulsion devices

Adaptive Divers who have use of their hands and arms can use underwater propulsion vehicles to propel themselves through the water. These UPV's are perfect for paraplegics, incomplete quadriplegics and other adaptive divers who have functional upper bodies but may have limited use of their lower extremities. Some UPV devices like the Pegasus thruster can be attached to the tank of an Adaptive Diver. Special training is required to safely use such devices and is beyond the scope of this training program,

Descent lines with buoy and anchor (used for divers requiring assistance with controlled descents/ascents & equalization)

For Adaptive Divers requiring assistance with controlled ascents/descents, Full-Face Mask use, equalization, or who may otherwise require more time to descend, using a descent line with a buoy and anchor adds a margin of safety and is recommended.

The descent line is particularly useful to adaptive diving since it helps the team descend and stop at desired depth with greater control. It is quite common that one or more team members will have different descent rates, and each member will likely need to stop and equalize at different times. The need for three divers to synchronize their equalization, buoyancy control and make the necessary adjustments during descents and ascents can be challenging.

In addition, as the team descends they are multi-tasking while focusing on the Adaptive Diver, coordinating several functions including, pinching nose pieces or manipulating Adaptive Diver's Full-Face Mask while equalizing, monitoring safe ascent/descent rates for the Adaptive Diver and themselves, establishing neutral buoyancy, operating the Adaptive Diver and their own BCD low pressure buttons, etc. The entire dive team may drift a considerable distance due to prevailing currents losing sight of the dive boat and dive site requiring a greater expenditure of energy swimming back against the current.

Having a descent line removes this potential problem enhancing the chances of having a more enjoyable and safe dive without exerting unnecessary energy and unduly burning tank air during the descent. One of your dive buddies can use a leg wrap on the line during the descent to help control the buoyancy for both of you. While secured to the line, his hands will be freed up to manipulate the buttons valves and levers used for BCD inflation and purging, for him and you, as well as, for equalization and signaling.

It should be used regardless of whether a current is initially present since currents are unpredictable and can develop within a short time and change directions without notice.

During training and other diving activities, the descent line also serves as a visual reference to help you and your dive team gauge ascent rates and is especially useful to help the team maintain the same depth during safety stops.

Regulator Necklace Holder (useful for divers requiring assistance with regulator recovery)

The regulator necklace holder is essentially a necklace made from a variety of materials (i.e. rubber, silicon, nylon straps, bungee cords, etc.) and designed to hold your regulator's 2nd stage mouthpiece to hang below your chin in the upper chest area. With this device you will always know where to find your regulator for easier recovery and retrieval should your regulator drop out of your mouth. This piece of adaptive gear is very useful to divers with upper mobility impairments. A diver who has limited functional arm movement may have enough physical capacity to successfully manipulate the regulator to his mouth from its secured position. It is also an effective device for blind divers enabling them to perform regulator recoveries independently without the need for team assistance.

Adaptive Diver Profile Slate

Just as pilots use the pre-flight safety check and divers use the predive safety check, Adaptive Dive teams should use the Adaptive Diver profile slate prior to any dive. The slate is a checklist that reminds us to be mindful of the myriad of things that have to be addressed when taking a diver with a disability underwater.

CHAPTER 7: DIVEHEART'S ADAPTIVE DIVER CERTIFICATIONS

With your Diveheart Adaptive Diver certification you will be able to enjoy diving throughout the world with the confidence and knowledge that you have been properly trained to scuba dive. Upon successful completion of your Adaptive Scuba course, you will be issued a Diveheart Adaptive Diver certification card that will not only verify you have successfully completed Diveheart's Adaptive Scuba Training Program but will also state the qualifications of your adaptive dive team and any adaptive equipment you may need to safely dive.

Diveheart believes that a Diveheart Adaptive Diver certification will prove to be the best way to mitigate the chances that a dive boat or dive shop operator will refuse to sell you a dive trip, fill your tanks or rent you equipment. At a minimum your certification card will be recognized by the many dive shops and operators that already recognize Diveheart as a leader in adaptive scuba training and will give you many opportunities to dive on Diveheart-sponsored trips, as well as the many dive trips offered by other adaptive dive organizations.

Adaptive Diver (AD) and Open Water Certifications (OW)

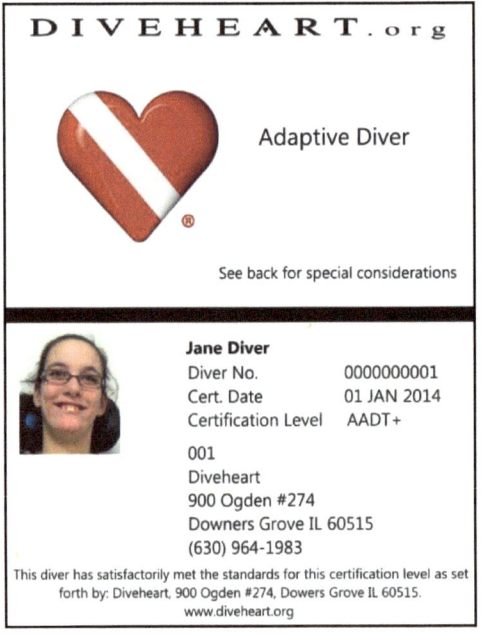

AD an OW certifications will be issued to divers who have successfully completed the course requirements of Diveheart and a nationally recognized scuba training agency. You will receive two certification cards; an open water certification card and Diveheart's Adaptive Diver certification. There will be NO conditions on the Diveheart certification card. You will be eligible to advance your training to become a certified Adaptive Dive Buddy, Adaptive Scuba Instructor or other additional training. You are uniquely qualified to make major contributions in establishing and creating greater awareness for adaptive scuba and making it more available to the community of individuals with disabilities.

Adaptive Diver - Adaptive Dive Team (ADT)

This certification will be issued to a diver who has successfully completed both the course requirements of Diveheart and a nationally recognized scuba training agency and the diver's NSA score was 25 or below. Your certification card will indicate that you are an Adaptive Diver whose buddy team must include two certified Adaptive Dive Buddies.

Adaptive Diver - Advanced Adaptive Dive Team (AADT)

This certification will be issued to a diver who has successfully completed both the course requirements of Diveheart and a nationally recognized scuba training agency and the diver's NSA score was above 25 or required assistance with: controlled ascents and descents, equalization, out of air emergency alternatives, and/or Full-Face Mask usage. Your certification card will indicate that you are an Adaptive Diver whose buddy team must include two Adaptive Dive Buddies certified by a nationally recognized adaptive scuba agency and one of the Adaptive Dive Buddies must have Diveheart's Advanced Adaptive Dive Buddy certification or a certified Adaptive Dive Buddy who has certifications equivalent to Diveheart's advanced certification.

Adaptive Diver - Advanced Adaptive Dive Team Plus special conditions (AADT +)

This certification will be issued to a diver who has successfully completed the course requirements of Diveheart and a nationally recognized scuba training agency (that grants limited open water certifications) and whose NSA score is greater than 25, or required assistance with controlled ascents and descents, equalization, out of air emergency alternatives, and/or Full-Face Mask usage, **and** requires some other special assistance, adaptation, procedures or equipment.

For example, if a family member or trusted friend is required to help reduce stress or provide emotional security throughout the dive for the diver, the certification card will indicate that such individuals must be part of the adaptive dive team. Such trusted friend or family member must also be a certified dive buddy and the other dive team member must be a certified DH adaptive instructor or be a certified adaptive instructor who has a certification equivalent to Diveheart's Adaptive Scuba Instructor certification.

Additionally, divers will receive this certification if they are unable to, or do not wish to, complete the entire open water course but want to complete one of the limited *entry level* scuba certifications. The Adaptive Diver must dive with an adaptive dive team that includes an Adaptive Scuba Instructor and one certified dive buddy and may only dive during daylight hours to a maximum depth of 40 feet.

Any other special adaptation, procedure, or equipment that is necessary to assist you to safely dive and perform required scuba skills will also be noted on this type of card as a condition or limitation to diving.

CHAPTER 8: IMAGINE THE POSSIBILITIES

When the idea of Diveheart was born in the 1980s, the original vision and mission was to use the *wonder of the water column* and its unique properties of zero gravity to build confidence, independence and self-esteem in children, adults and veterans with disabilities. We had no idea that we would be ushering in a new era of rehabilitation for the body, mind and spirit that would come to be called "Scuba Therapy".

Whether you were born with a disability, or acquired a disability through a traumatic event, you have learned to adjust to a "New Normal" that may be different from people around you. Diveheart uses Scuba Therapy to help them make this transition.

Once an individual experiences zero gravity underwater with Diveheart, it gives them new perspective on life. It creates a paradigm shift in the individual and a new identity. It's no longer Johnny in the wheelchair, it's "Johnny the scuba diver." Johnny now looks at himself differently and others around him look at him differently too. "If I can scuba dive, I can do anything" he says. Johnny then takes on challenges he might never have taken on before. Johnny has begun the journey. With his new found confidence, independence and self esteem, he now can "Imagine the Possibilities" in his life.

You may ask …why and how does zero gravity and Scuba Therapy work? What makes this experience so powerful, so different from other therapies?

Let's start with the idea of a human being going underwater and breathing. This of course is not natural, but is possible through scuba and hooka/snooba or other forms of surface supplied air. Just the idea of going underwater and breathing is scary for many "able-bodied individuals". Some people have claustrophobia, fear of water, fear of fish and of course fear of sharks.

Because of these fears or conditions and because most of the world's bodies of water are either cold and murky, not easily accessible or are too expensive to get to, less than one percent of the world's population dives. Having said that, most people are fascinated with the thought of scuba diving and the excitement, adventure and danger that surrounds it. The popular image of a diver is certainly not that of someone with a disability or someone in a wheelchair. That image is changing thanks to the efforts of organizations like Diveheart.

It is the perception by the vast majority of nondivers that in order to be a scuba diver you have to be able bodied, physically fit and fearless. That is precisely why it is a powerful tool that we can use to change the popular perception that people with disabilities are incapable of or shouldn't be able to dive.

When Johnny rolls into a party or family function and someone asks "So what did you do this summer Johnny?" and he answers that he spent a week on a scuba adventure trip with Diveheart, many jaws drop in awe. "How can you scuba dive"? Maybe Johnny is in a wheelchair, or is blind or has a traumatic brain injury or amputation. In many minds Johnny is certainly not a candidate for scuba diving.

Johnny's new identity will turn heads, widen eyes and surprise many friends and family. This new identity will give him the opportunity to reshape his world by changing the perceptions of others. Perceptions surrounding Johnny's abilities. With his new found confidence, independence and self esteem, Johnny can focus on what he can do, not what he can't do and it will keep him moving forward, not backwards.

At Diveheart we know that just one pool session can change someone's life regardless of whether they have autism, cerebral palsy or a spinal cord injury. With tools like social media and easy ways to capture underwater videos and photos, we can give someone a life changing experience from just one session in the pool. Johnny can now go home and post his videos and photos, showing off his new identity online and share it with his circle of friends and family or the world.

After a CNN/Headline News crew spent a week with Diveheart and a group of veterans with disabilities in the Florida Keys, producer Bryan Simmons walked up to Diveheart founder Jim Elliott and said. "I get it now. Scuba Divers are the poor man's astronaut". Elliott said "Bryan, I'm totally using that line, because it's right on the money, we are the poor man's astronaut".

Environment

Once Diveheart creates a paradigm shift in the person with a disability, we then focus them on the environment working in tandem with marine parks around the world. The marine parks develop a curriculum that allows the new Adaptive Diver to help with local environmental projects like coral reef restoration, marine biology and oceanography.

Imagine the potential to help the environment and the individual by making that person a good steward of the environment. Not to mention how it will help the local economy if their efforts result in healthier more vibrant reefs for tourist divers and snorkelers to visit.

Research

At least a hundred years of research lies before us as therapists develop new techniques in the zero gravity environment underwater. Diveheart is working with researchers at university medical centers like Duke and Midwestern University to understand more about how the combination of pressure and zero gravity might benefit children with autism or veterans with spinal cord injuries or traumatic brain injuries.

The anecdotal evidence that Diveheart has seen to date suggests that individuals with a wide variety of abilities will benefit from scuba therapy.

We believe the introduction of mixed gas and pure oxygen at shallow depths combined with scuba therapy will introduce a new level of research that will realize medical benefits we have not yet dreamed of.

Not to discount other therapies and types of research but with scuba therapy, we will have the franchise on zero gravity. This is something that has never been done before on earth.

Vision

It is Diveheart's vision to conduct much of the research, rehabilitation, education, training and vocational work in a warm deep water therapy pool that will give researchers the benefit of a controlled, confined water environment. This facility will draw the best and the brightest from around the world in medical research, therapy, aerospace and the sciences.

Forget the moon; "Inner Space" is where the next frontier is waiting. We will be able to help individuals of all abilities through zero gravity underwater and it will be a fraction of what NASA spends to experience zero gravity in outer space. Some people say there is nothing new under the sun, but they are wrong. Scuba Therapy is new and zero gravity is going to pioneer in a new age of research and therapy that will revolutionize rehabilitation for people of all abilities.

It is our belief at Diveheart that scuba therapy will benefit the young and old as well as individuals struggling with obesity issues. The benefits to the body, mind and spirit will be awesome. Veterans transitioning back from combat with disabilities and post traumatic stress disorder are at enormous risk of depression, substance abuse and suicide. Perhaps scuba therapy will not cure those problems in their entirety, but it can give veterans with disabilities purpose and value again. Whether it's a pool program or a shark dive, there is something in zero gravity for every veteran who joins us in our journey and we believe that scuba therapy can help stem the tide of suicide among the ranks of our servicemen and women. We believe resources need to be directed now to help grow these opportunities for veterans with disabilities.

What we do is not about scuba diving, it's about using zero gravity as a tool to inspire those with disabilities to imagine the possibilities in their lives. We all need to be loved, be valued and have a purpose, and the endless opportunities that exist in zero gravity for those with disabilities will give them that purpose, a reason to get up in the morning.

Scuba instructors have been adapting scuba skills for years to accommodate their students with special needs. Diveheart is just moving it to another level. Diveheart's successful promotion of adaptive scuba has led to every major training agency offering some form of adaptive scuba program to its customers. Diveheart's marketing of the business of adaptive scuba has shown retailers and training agencies alike that the growth of the scuba industry lies in scuba therapy.

Awareness is always the challenge. The last thing someone with a disability is thinking is "Let's go scuba diving". We know it's probably one of the most powerful things they can do to heal their body, mind and spirit.

ABOUT DIVEHEART

Less than one percent of the world's population has tried scuba diving. Less than one percent of the diving community works with people with disabilities. A very small percentage of that adaptive dive community works with individuals with virtually any disability and only one organization does all of the above and promotes and facilitates adaptive scuba, the business of adaptive scuba and ground-breaking research surrounding scuba therapy, around the world. That organization is Diveheart.

After launching programs in China, Australia, Israel, the UK, all over the Caribbean and in more than two hundred cities around the U.S., Diveheart has inspired thousands of divers and instructors around the world to "Imagine the Possibilities" for individuals of all abilities in their communities. This has led to the creation of twenty additional non-profit organizations that

Diveheart has helped to develop. These organizations work with individuals with disabilities and help spread the word about the power of adaptive scuba and scuba therapy.

Diveheart's work with children, adults and veterans with disabilities has led it to launch programs for children with autism in Israel, veterans with disabilities in the UK and active Marines and Navy corpsmen at Camp Pendleton and other military personnel at bases and veterans hospitals around the U.S.

Since 2001 Diveheart has been pioneering new and innovative training and adaptive diving techniques to make the Adaptive Dive experience safer and more fulfilling while growing the knowledge and experience base for adaptive buddies and instructors.

The Diveheart Adaptive Diver Certification program represents the latest innovations in adaptive scuba techniques, training and thinking. We believe that the Diveheart program is going to revolutionize adaptive scuba training around the world for instructors, dive buddies and adaptive divers of all abilities.

Diveheart's visibility and reputation in the dive community around the world will also help the Adaptive Diver when they travel to resorts and far away dive locations. Dive operators will know when you present the Diveheart certification card to them that you have undergone the most thorough adaptive scuba training in the world.

APPENDIX

Adaptive Diver Registry

Rev. Jan 26 2014

Date: _____

Event: _____

Location: _____

To Be Completed By Adaptive Diver, Parent or Guardian

Adaptive Diver Information:

Name: _____

D.O.B _____ WT. _____ HT _____

Shoe Size: _____ Clothing Size: SM   M   LG   XL   XXL

Address: _____

_____

Tel #: _____

Mobile #: _____

Email: _____

Emergency Contact:

Name: _____

Address: _____

_____

Tel#: _____

Mobile #: _____

Email: _____

Medical Clearance Physician Information:

Name: _____

Address: _____

_____

Tel#: _____

Mobile #: _____

Email: _____

On-site or Boat caregiver:

Name: _____

Address: _____

_____

Tel#: _____

Mobile #: _____

Email: _____

Medical History:

Describe your general health and any medical condition which impacts, to any extent, your activities of daily living and/or which you believe may affect your ability to SCUBA dive:

_____

_____

_____

Date of initial onset of such medical condition:_____

Describe specifically any physical impairment you may have:

_____

_____

Describe specifically any cognitive, psychological and/ or emotional impairment you may have:

_____

_____

_____

Do you currently have any open skin wounds?   Yes   No

Have you ever had a seizure?   Yes   No

If Yes, date of last seizure: _____

Are you on any anti-seizure medication?   Yes   No

Have you ever suffered from autonomic dysreflexia?   Yes   No

Hearing: (circle one)   deaf hard of hearing
hearing aid   N/A

Vision: (circle one) blind   visually impaired   glasses

contacts   N/A

Visual acuity without glasses_____

Do you use any medical devices related to your condition: (*Circle all that apply*)

Walking canes   Left arm: prosthetics/ brace

Right arm: prosthetics/ brace

Blind canes   Left Leg: prosthetics / brace

Right Leg: prosthetics / brace

Walkers   Wheelchairs   Drainage bag (s)

Other devices and/or supplies:

_____

_____

_____

Current Medications:

_____

_____

_____

SWIMMING SKILLS & EXPERIENCE:

Can you swim and tread water: Yes / No

Can you snorkel Dive: Yes / No

Past SCUBA Experience & Certifications:

Have you ever participated in a Discover SCUBA event (an event where you were introduced and experienced scuba in a pool or elsewhere)? Yes / No
Location:_____
Date:_____

Are you certified in SCUBA?   YES / NO   If yes; please provide the certification date: _____ ; and name of SCUBA training agency (Diveheart, HSA, PADI, etc.): _____.

Were you certified in SCUBA prior to your disability or physical impairment? YES / NO

Provide level of certification: _____

Date of last scuba dive? _____

Circle one: pool / open water

Total number of scuba dives in a pool, open water, quarry, etc. (lifetime)? _____

VERIFICATION:

I, _____, (Adaptive Diver), have reviewed the above registry information and verify that all the information set forth above is true and correct.

Signature_____

Date: _____

Print Name _____
Date: _____

I,_____, the natural parent or legal guardian of the above identified Adaptive Diver, have reviewed the above registry information and verify that all the information set forth above is true and correct.

Signature_____

Date: _____

Print Name _____
Date: _____

Needed Scuba Assistance- Student's Self Assessment

The information solicited in this registry and the <u>N</u>eeded <u>S</u>cuba <u>A</u>ssistance (NSA) -- Student-Self Assessment evaluation and score is designed to enable Diveheart to generally assess the special needs, adaptations and assistance you may require to perform scuba skills and related activities.

SCORING INSTRUCTIONS:

    This is a self-assessment and intended as a starting point in assessing your abilities to dive and how much, if any, assistance you may require. You should perform the NSA self assessment **after** you have reviewed and understand the course materials that describe how scuba skills are performed. For example, after you understand how to perform a mask clearing skill, you will need to assess whether or not you will need assistance in performing the skill. Base your answers to the following questions on your knowledge of your abilities and any physical impairment you may have .Your adaptive scuba instructor will perform his own assessment, but will consider your assessment to get a sense of how you view your own abilities

    Circle only one of the numerical values that correspond to each of the special needs and scuba skills below. If you do not believe you will require any assistance for any of items below, circle "0". If you "may" require assistance with the scuba skill, circle the value found in the middle column. If you believe you "do" require assistance, circle the value found in the third column. Add each item's assessment score to arrive at a total NSA score.

    If you are unsure if you "may" or "do" require assistance, please circle the higher value. You and your Adaptive Scuba Instructor will have the opportunity to revise your score once you have completed the training.

==Special Note: In order to assess whether you may need to use a Full-Face Mask please read pages 74 & 127 of your Diveheart training manual, sections entitled "Full-Face Mask" and "Diveheart's Mandatory Rules for Full Face Mask Usage".==

KEY SCUBA SKILLS: **Assistance -Levels:**

		No	May	Do
1	Full Face Mask Usage	0	3	6
2	Controlled descents and ascents	0	3	6
3	Equalization (ear and mask)	0	3	6
4	Out of air emergency alternatives	0	3	6

Special Needs- Precautions:

5	Monitoring of Autonomic Dysreflexia	0	.5	1
6	Transfers	0	.5	1
7	Thermal regulation protections	0	.5	1
8	Skin Protection	0	.5	1
9	Pressure sore protection	0	.5	1
10	Surface and U/W swimming	0	.5	1
11	UW communications signs & audible signals	0	.5	1

| 12 | Leg Bag and catheter precaution | 0 | .5 | 1 |

Basic Scuba Skills:

13	Diving system assembly and disassembly (at water's edge)	0	.5	1
14	Donning and removing scuba equipment and apparel topside	0	.5	1
15	Equipment inspection (at water's edge)	0	.5	1
16	Entries and exits	0	.5	1
17	Proper weighting	0	.5	1
18	Mouthpiece clearing--snorkel and regulator	0	.5	1
19	Regulator/snorkel exchanges at the surface	0	.5	1
20	Underwater swimming	0	.5	1
21	Mask-clearing	0	.5	1
22	Mask removal and replacement	0	.5	1
23	Buddy-system techniques	0	.5	1
24	Diver assistance techniques (self/buddy/group)	0	.5	1
25	Surface-snorkel swimming with full diving system	0	.5	1

26	Regulator recovery/retrieval	0	.5	1
27	Regulator clearing	0	.5	1
28	Underwater removal and replacement of the weight/ballast system	0	.5	1
29	Removal and replacement of scuba system	0	.5	1
30	Equipment care and maintenance (at the water's edge)	0	.5	1
31	Underwater navigation	0	.5	1

Total NSA Score: _____

www.ingramcontent.com/pod-product-compliance
Lightning Source LLC
Chambersburg PA
CBHW041430300426
44114CB00002B/19